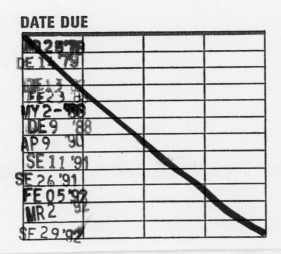

The Conscience of a Young Conservative

The Conscience of a Young Conservative

DONALD LAMBRO

ARLINGTON HOUSE·PUBLISHERS
NEW ROCHELLE, NEW YORK

ISBN 0-87000-344-5

Manufactured in the United States of America

Library of Congress Cataloging in Publication Data

Lambro, Donald.
    The conscience of a young conservative.

    1. The United States—Politics and government—1945–
2. United States—Economic policy—1961
3. United States—Social policy. I. Title.
JK271.L26   309.1'73'092   76-10147
ISBN 0-87000-334-5

For Jason

Contents

Introduction

Americans are deeply troubled about the direction their country has taken. They sense that something has gone wrong, terribly wrong.

Government at every level has grown enormously, yet taxpayers doubt they are getting any more for their tax dollar than they did twenty years ago. People are earning more, but more of their income is being taken from them by local, state, and federal taxes. Our police, teachers, and civil servants are being paid better than ever, but crime continues to soar, public education is failing, and government is becoming less and less responsive to the people.

Pollster Louis Harris recently found that 67 percent of all Americans believe that "what you think doesn't count much anymore." An almost identical percentage agreed with the statement that "the people running the country don't care what happens to you." Harris also found that 72 percent of the people do not think they receive their money's worth from their tax dollars.

More significant is the fact that Congress, the courts, the presidency, and

9

other political institutions have sunk to all-time lows in public esteem and confidence. The Harris poll revealed that confidence in doctors is down to 44 percent from 72 percent. In higher education it is down to 33 percent from 61 percent. Organized labor was down to 14 percent from 22 percent. The military fell to 29 percent from 62 percent. Congress plunged down to 13 percent from 42 percent, and the executive branch sank to 13 percent from 43 percent. Confidence in local government leaders was lower still, plummeting to 7 percent. At the top of the heap, so to speak, were garbage collectors, who maintained the greatest confidence of the people. Harris found that people gave them high marks because at least they knew whether or not their trash was being taken away!

Despite such deeply held skepticism and loss of confidence, a majority of Americans continue to accept the same tired and redundant "solutions" liberals have been offering for decades—the creation of still more government to deal with age-old problems: poverty, crime, illiteracy, inflation, and social unrest. But these and other problems remain. In many respects they have gotten worse, much worse. All the rosy rhetoric in the world can't dismiss this alarming and impregnable truth. Incredibly, however, that truth has never been fully and effectively driven home to the American people.

The principal aim of this book is to point out graphically where we've gone wrong. To demonstrate there are limits to how much hard-earned income can be taken from Americans and spent by government on programs they don't want—and can't afford. To show that much of government is wasteful, self-perpetuating, and in many respects highly elitist. To show that government is, in bits and pieces, diminishing our liberties, consuming what vestiges remain of our privacy and freedom. To show that our economy has been severely shackled by government, to the point where federal regulation and taxation are unnecessarily costing consumers tens of billions of dollars every year. To detail how, in our zeal for more social welfare programs, we've gone far beyond what we can afford. To suggest in the cold light of crime statistics a harsh but sensible alternative to an endemic problem. To look at federal education programs and show that there are no clear policies, but, instead, a tangle of experimental and often warped "education" programs that are turning out a class of educationally underdeveloped Americans. To survey America's military defenses and show that we can rid our Defense Department of vast waste as well as dealing with critical deficiencies in our armed capabilities. And, finally, to look at American foreign policy as it exists "in the real world" and to suggest what our country should stand for around the globe,

In sum, this is a political essay for the last half of the 1970s. It is a critique of liberal practices and policies as we have known them since the 1930s, focusing particularly on what our government has wrought over the past fifteen years.

My conclusion? The liberal or so-called progressive approach to domestic problems has failed miserably—so miserably that, on the state level at least, governors are rushing one by one from its prevailing dogmas into the more comforting arms of fiscal restraint and limited government (in one form or another). From California to Maine, state chief executives are staking their political futures on holding down the size and cost of government. One need look only at New York City's dismal plight to see what happens when government leaders think the sky's the limit and set their policies for the sole purpose of winning elections.

In the field of foreign policy we are shifting from a position of strength to a position of weakness, totally ignoring the moral imperatives that should be at the very core of every policy we pursue around the globe.

After over a decade of political reporting, I am convinced that liberals succeed in selling their schemes year after year, election after election, in large part because of their skillful exploitation of the art of political attack. It is not so much their proposals that have drawn popular support (which, of course, they have to a degree), but fear of the boogymen they have so cleverly crafted to frighten the people into accepting greater government involvement in their daily lives. The specters of big oil, unscrupulous bankers, sinister middlemen, profiteering corporations, evil lobbyists, and nuclear holocausts are raised one after the other to pressure Americans into accepting the liberals' largely collectivist concepts.

To a degree, this book is an informal examination of some of these liberal boogymen. It is primarily, however, an examination of several major areas of government concern that attempts to show where government has gone wrong and where it shouldn't have gotten involved in the first place. It also raises a few alternatives that for one reason or another are not being broached in the chambers and council rooms of official Washington.

What I hope this book will accomplish is to convince the reader that our country is set upon a disastrous course in a multitude of areas, political and social, and that big government at home and unprincipled weakness abroad are not the answers. They are the problems.

I

Government

The Money Hungry Bureaucracy

Government is exploding. Faster than the economy that must pay for it. Faster than taxpayers can keep up with its demands for their earnings.

In fact, government at all levels—federal, state, and local—has literally gotten out of control, collecting and redistributing 44 percent of our national income.

Over the past ten years state and local spending has skyrocketed some 204 percent, more than one-and-a-half times the gross national product for the same period. State and local employment rose 60 percent in the last decade, about twice the rate of all wage and salary workers. The combined debt of state and local governments went up 118 percent, twice the increase in the federal debt for the same period.

The federal budget, meanwhile, has been blazing out of control, with a 38 percent increase from fiscal year 1974 to fiscal 1976. Since 1960 domestic federal spending has spun upward more than seven times faster than the population. Over the past fifteen years federal spending for direct income or benefits for individuals, adjusted for inflation, has been rising

13

about 7.8 percent each year, more than twice as fast as the GNP. In other words, federal domestic spending has been growing at twice the rate of the economy that must provide the money to pay for such spending.

In fiscal year 1966 federal spending outlays totaled $134.7 billion. By fiscal 1974 they had doubled to $268.4 billion. Outlays shot to $324.6 billion in fiscal 1975 and were expected to rise to $375 billion or higher in fiscal 1976.

Clearly, our national government is living far beyond its means, racking up bigger and bigger deficits with each succeeding year. The U.S. Treasury has had deficits in fifteen of the past sixteen years. In fiscal year 1975 the federal government spent $44.21 billion more than it took in. This was the biggest budget deficit in thirty years. In fiscal 1976 the deficit was expected to hit $75-80 billion. Interest payments on the national debt for the same year were estimated to be over $37.5 billion. The gross federal debt was expected to go over $625.5 billion.

Although President Ford declared he was "horrified" at having to propose a fiscal 1975 budget of $359 billion—which was gradually pushed up to $370 billion—the bureaucracy over which he vainly sought to exert some control propelled his fiscal 1977 budget requests to almost $400 billion.

The incredible speed with which federal spending is being pushed upward is difficult to comprehend. America needed 185 years to reach the $100 billion level in federal spending, but only nine more years to hit the $200 billion mark, and just four more years to achieve $300 billion. It took only two additional years to pole-vault over $400 billion.

Knowing the speed at which spending is rising, it takes little imagination to see where we are going. Someone, sometime, is going to have to pay for all this. And that someone is the beleaguered American taxpayer and consumer.

Treasury Secretary William Simon once observed that "in a very real sense, we have been living off our inheritance and mortgaging our future. We have transferred more and more of our wealth out of the most productive part of our economy, the private sector, and into the least productive part, the government."

America's vast wealth has become one huge mortgage payment in an endless sea of debt. Writer-economist Richard Whalen knows what America's finances rest upon:

> In a word: debt. Debt so unimaginably large in the private sector and public sectors alike—some $2.5 trillion, according to the latest count—that the idea of ever paying off any substantial part of it is unthinkable. McGraw-Hill's economists recently totalled up the categories: $1 trillion in corporate debt, $600 billion in mortgage debt, $600 billion in U.S. government debt, $200 billion in state and local government debt, and $200 billion in consumer debt. Merely to pay the interest due this year [1975], they calculated, would take a sum more than one-third the GNP of the next biggest capitalist economy, Japan.

President Ford has declared that "ever increasing government spending for all social programs literally threatens our whole economy." Representative Robert Michel of Illinois, the House Republican Whip, warned that "unless we in Congress do something about it, we're headed toward a first-class fiscal disaster." The wise economists predict that, if spending grows at the rate of the past twenty years, half of America will be living off the other half by the year 2000. Observed columnist George F. Will, "But that is the American way. If you're going, go first-class, even if where you're going is just deeper into debt."

Unfortunately, there are people in America who are unconcerned about the nation's fiscal dilemma. It isn't their debt and they will not be held responsible for the consequences. These are the people who believe that government should spend and borrow whatever is necessary to pay for the programs to which they are ideologically committed. George Meany, president of the AFL-CIO, lectured Congress that it should be concerned with only one goal, meeting "the needs of the American people. If meeting those needs adds up to a [fiscal year] 1976 deficit of $80 or $90 or $100 billion—so be it: and, if more is required, then more should be provided." *Washington Post* economic writer Hobart Rowen, dismissing Ford's anti–big spending speeches as "a tired echo of the 1930's," argued that "in many ways and places, local and national government is corrupt, venal and wasteful, even dumb. . . . But in the real world, big government is here to stay."

15

Meany and Rowen's tribulations conjure up New York City Mayor Robert Wagner's stubborn declaration in his 1965 budget message: "I do not propose to permit our fiscal problems to set the limits of our commitments to meet the essential needs of the people of the city." The tremors of Manhattan's coming bankruptcy could even then be felt, if only barely. Wagner and his friends were going to save the city if it took every last penny the people had.

There are those in Washington, too, who are prepared to spend and borrow to continue old programs and initiate new ones if it takes every last cent you have. And our obese bureaucracy on the Potomac has an insatiable appetite. It takes a hefty 799-page manual for the government to explain its vast structure, now composed of more than 3500 agencies, departments, divisions, boards, commissions, corporations, services, authorities, councils, and other assorted bureaucracies. Close to three million civilian employees balloon the bureaucracy, and their numbers—like inflation statistics—continue to rise.

When Ford took office in August, 1974, federal civilian workers numbered about 2,866,904. By July, 1975, their numbers had risen to 2,930,849—an infusion of 63,945 new employees in a little over eleven months. New federal employees were propagated in almost every major agency, with ten of eleven Cabinet-level departments growing fatter. The Treasury was up 7423 employees to 124,898. Health, Education and Welfare had an increase of 7340 workers, for a total of 149,364. The Defense Department racked up 1,051,679 civilian employees, up 4455. The Federal Communications Commission was up from 1992 to 2121. The Interstate Commerce Commission up from 1970 to 2091, the Securities and Exchange Commission from 1910 to 2001.

Three new agencies created under the Ford administration were among the biggest employers in the government. The Federal Energy Administration bulged with 3245 employees, the Nuclear Regulatory Commission, 2300. And the Energy Research and Development Administration quickly filled its payroll with 8262 workers.

Parkinson's law states that any given number of workers can be counted on to produce exactly enough work needed to fill their time. In the federal bureaucracy that means paperwork—billions upon billions of duplicate, triplicate, and what-licate documents and forms. The National Archives once tried to count every type of federal form and stopped after they had reached the one million mark. "We just gave up," an Archives official told me. "We thought we had proved our point."

Washington is drowning America in paperwork. Consumers, businessmen, taxpayers, homebuyers, all are being smothered by government forms—census forms, tax forms, safety forms, health forms, employment forms, contract forms, compliance forms, all of which cost our economy an estimated $40 billion a year to fill out, process, and maintain. It is estimated that there are ten different government forms for every man, woman, and child in America and that the flow of paper fills four and a half million cubic feet of government space each year. The General Accounting Office says federal files would stretch the 5600 miles from Washington to Cairo.

When Senator William Proxmire of Wisconsin asked government agencies to send him a copy of every form they used, the reaction was one of bemused frustration and utter shock. Proxmire might just as well have asked a confetti manufacturer to send him a copy of everything he had produced since day one. "My God," a Census Bureau official replied. "It would take three people two days just to pull all the forms."

An exasperated HEW Secretary David Mathews said, "If we start now and work until doomsday, we could never get all the forms together."

"You know what everyone did when I told them of your request?" an Internal Revenue Service official asked Proxmire. "They laughed!"

Oddly, very little of all this paperwork is ever thrown away. Archives officials have said that 40 percent of the government's inactive files could be thrown out, but they could persuade agencies to destroy only 8 percent. The cost to taxpayers for the government to handle, manage, and store all of this paper? Over $8 billion a year.

Congress, who created the programs that in turn produced this avalanche of paper, is largely to blame for this mess. More than 9000 laws require reports and filings of one type or another. Between 1965 and 1968, when Congress was practically salivating over President Johnson's Great Society binge, the number of governnent administrative and statistical reports grew by 30 percent. That trend continues today.

The question is, Why Do We Need All This Government? What is it really doing for us? Could we get by with a lot less, allowing Americans to keep a greater share of their earnings? Over the past fifteen years, 236 new federal agencies, bureaus, and commissions have been created by Congress. Only twenty-one have been abolished. Even a cursory survey of all that the federal government does makes clear that Americans are paying for more government than they need. Through decades of "activist" government, during which Congress enacted program after program and created agency upon agency, our government has grown all out of proportion to America's needs and income. It has grown so large and so fast that no one man or institution within that government can truthfully say the bureaucracy is being run by anyone or anything. A leviathan out of control, it runs itself—at our expense.

Frustrated presidents have been unable to bring the bureaucratic infrastructure under control. Congress, through its oversight and appropriations committees, can only probe the fringes of the monstrous departments it has created, rarely delving beneath the bloated multibillion-dollar line items in the budget to see where all of our money is really going.

"Most of it is out of control," a Senate Appropriations Committee staffer once confided to me. "Most of these guys don't know what the hell they're voting on. And fewer still understand where all of this money is being spent."

If a panel of average Americans, selected at random from the telephone books of ten major metropolitan areas, were to spend a week touring Washington's vast network of government corridors and offices, they would be shocked. There are hundreds, perhaps thousands, of programs and governmental agencies that are totally ineffective, duplicative, unnecessary, extravagant, or simply outdated. So many programs have been piled on top of other programs that we've forgotten what's underneath, which all too often is duplicating what's on top. In eleven Cabinet-level departments and thirty-six independent agencies we are juggling a system of over 1000 grants-in-aid programs. There are 228 programs in the health field alone, requiring ten different agencies to administer them. A General Accounting Office study pinpointed 186 programs scatterred over twenty federal agencies—all providing funds for community development.

Still more examples of duplication include seven separate programs providing funds for outpatient health facilities, eleven different programs providing money for child care, and fourteen separate HEW programs administering programs to educate the handicapped. There are at least twenty-five separate organizations, scattered among a dozen different departments and agencies, conducting research into water pollution.

The nooks and crannies of the federal structure harbor 1307 federal advisory boards, committees, commissions, councils, and panels fueled and run by some 4000 federal employees so that we might enjoy the benefits of a Plant Variety Protection Board, a Dance Advisory Panel, a Personality and Cognition Research Review Committee, and a National Board for the Promotion of Rifle Practice.

Decade after decade we tolerate maintaining the status quo among our regulatory agencies, despite proof that they prohibit and interfere with the very competitive practices that result in lower consumer costs and smother innovation that could mean more efficient service—not to mention the millions of dollars they add to our tax burden. The Civil Aeronautics Board and the Interstate Commerce Commission are just two of the regulatory agencies that economists say are costing consumers billions of dollars a year more for virtually everything they buy.

Our government is spending over $1 billion a year on public relations. A survey by the Associated Press found 6391 full- and part-time public relations, or "information," officers on the federal payroll. Government flackery has become one of Washington's major industries, with the federal puff mill each year grinding out millions of press releases and countless books, magazines, pamphlets, movies, and radio and television broadcasts. The Defense Department alone has a $24.5 million worldwide public relations operation requiring 1518 PR employees. The Department of Health, Education and Welfare employs more than 1000 "public affairs" people. The Agriculture Department maintains a PR staff of 600. The Labor Depprtment has 145 PR types. Interior has 124, seven of whom work only on the "Johnny Horizon" antilitter advertisements. The Justice Department uses 28 PR men. Without a doubt, three-fourths of the government's Madison Avenue corps is unnecessary.

There are about 5,014,161 people now on the federal payroll; 2,166,500 are military. At the beginning of 1975, the total federal payroll was costing taxpayers about $70 billion a year. Postal pay raises agreed to in 1975 plus the 5 percent pay hike Congress approved for itself, the military, the judiciary, and white collar civil service employees from the vice president on down shot the federal payroll to about $74 billion a year—all of it being paid for with *borrowed* money. Cracked one Washingtonian, "Who do we think we are, New York City?"

In 1929 one out of sixteen persons was a government worker. In 1947 the ratio was one out of ten. In 1967, one out of six. And in 1972, one out of five. At this rate, by the year 2049 we'll all be working for government.

Nothing better illustrates the incredible growth of our government than the food stamp program, which began as a pilot project in 1961 with 50,000 recipients and is now totally out of control—providing food stamps for more than 19 million people at a cost of almost $6 billion a year.

How much is being wasted through food-stamp fraud or overpayments? A *Washington Star* projection using the Agriculture Department's own quality control study figures indicated that $797 million in food stamps were paid to ineligible people or in overpayments. If this estimate is accurate, one food stamp program dollar in six was misspent. Some Agriculture and HEW officials say that closer to one out of five food stamp dollars (nearly $800 million) is being misspent.

The extent of fraud is more difficult to assess. Fraud charges were brought against 34,000 stamp users in the last year. The *Star*'s probe concluded that "If the error rate, which has remained virtually constant for the past two years, continues at the same pace this fiscal year, the taxpayers could lose an additional $983 million in overpayments or payments to ineligible persons due to mistakes, bureaucratic bungling and deliberate cheating."

Our federal pension system allows 100,000 "double dippers" to annually rake in their government pension while holding another federal job, adding about $600 million a year to government pension costs. The government's four retirement and pension systems presently have an unfunded liability approaching $500 billion, including veterans compensation and pensions, Civil Service, and military and railroad retirement. Not only are the double dippers collecting both their government pension plus their federal pay, but they also receive automatic cost-of-living increases.

20

According to the National Taxpayers Union, some double dippers are collecting $50,000 or more while "retired" on the federal payroll. Sid Taylor, NTU research director, once observed that giving pay raises to this group of federal employees—who received a 5 percent pay hike in 1975—"is like sending food stamps to J. Paul Getty." In 1975 there were thirty-eight double dippers in Congress alone.

The federal retirement funds are becoming a trillion dollar monstrosity. The military retirement fund currently has an actuarial deficit, or unfunded liability, of some $169 billion. The Civil Service Retirement Fund deficit adds about $90 billion. The veterans compensation and pension fund is about $186 billion in the red, while the Railroad Retirement Fund now is some $9 billion in debt. Adding it all up, there is a total taxpayer unfunded liability of at least $454 billion in federal retirement fund deficits, and this is *in addition to* the national debt of over $600 billion.

"To get the full picture," the NTU's Taylor said,

> our national debt plus financial commitments and fiscal liabilities now total over $5 trillion! It's time we recognized our "economic Pearl Harbor" and began to fight deficit spending and wage our real war on inflation. We can't spend ourselves out of inflation. This is like drinking yourself out of alcoholism. We are about to get cirrhosis of the Treasury. The only cure is for government, business, and labor to produce more, and to price themselves back into the market. Failing this, the taxpayers' 1976 bumper sticker should read: Deficit Spending is Bankruptcy Pending.

The massive Social Security system went into the red for the first time in 1975. The fund's long-range deficit projections into the next century may be nearly double earlier estimates. Social Security was anticipated to pay out almost $3 billion more in 1975 than the system collected. The latest seventy-five-year projection anticipates an annual average deficit of 5.3 percent. Unless Social Security taxes are raised or a cap is placed on future benefits, the $46.1 billion trust fund will be depleted by 1981. Congress has been so reckless in approving increased benefits under the system, and passing the tab along to struggling single and married wage earners, that outlays have been promised all out of proportion to the system's capacity to pay on a fiscally sound basis.

21

At times it almost seems as if the federal government is incapable of using money either wisely or economically, whether spending it or saving it. One government audit found that it cost the government an additional $57 billion on 269 federal construction projects because of cost overruns. The overruns ballooned original cost estimates 75 percent, from $76 billion to $133 billion. The study found that costs of fifty-nine of the nonmilitary construction projects—which accounted for $46 billion of the overrun total—swelled from at least two to nearly nine times original estimates.

Meanwhile, it was revealed in late 1974 that our government was keeping an average of $4 billion in noninterest-paying accounts at commercial banks throughout the country—losing $428 million in potential interest, or more than $1 million a day. The income lost to the government would have been enough—according to *Washington Post* investigative reporter Ronald Kessler—to run four major federal regulatory agencies plus the Smithsonian Institution, the Secret Service, the Senate, and the Supreme Court for one full year.

Hardly a month goes by that we do not read how the multibillion dollar Department of Housing and Urban Development is paying hundreds of millions of dollars to bail out housing subsidy programs. In 1974 HUD was spending $2 billion annually to save programs swamped with defaults on federally insured mortgages. Yet, for all the billions the government has spent through HUD, the fact remains that the housing industry has remained in a slump and will continue to do poorly as long as rising federal deficit spending removes billions in investment capital from the private sector.

A mild recovery in housing starts in the summer of 1975 suffered a setback as a result of disintermediation, or the flow of money out of savings banks due to higher interest returns elsewhere. A prime factor in this process was the U.S. Treasury. The irresistible yields of 8 percent or more from Treasury issues drew money out of savings institutions, money which otherwise would have gone to provide mortgages. The supply of money available for housing loans was restricted and higher interest rates resulted.

All the emergency housing subsidy programs and efforts to legislate lower interest rates are not going to stimulate the housing market. They will only make the problem worse. The housing industry is going to respond

22

when the capital is there in sufficient quantity for mortgage loans at rates that the average American can afford.

Inflation is pricing housing beyond the reach of the average prospective homeowner. And Washington's spending and borrowing policies are the single most aggravating cause of inflation. Senator Jake Garn of Utah is one of the few members of the Senate who understands both the problem and its cure: "It doesn't take a brilliant economist to know that when government needs money, it borrows it from the private sector, crowds out those who would borrow it to build, develop or buy and forces up construction costs and mortgage interest rates. It is, in fact, the federal government that is causing the nation's housing woes."

Incredibly, despite a sharp drop in federally assisted housing and heavy cuts in federal urban development programs, HUD's spending has nearly doubled since 1972. In fact, since fiscal 1972, total HUD spending has risen from $3.6 billion to an estimated $7.1 billion in fiscal 1976. During this same period the number of HUD-assisted housing starts for low- and moderate-income families plummeted from 338,000 units to an estimated 188,000 units, twenty-two assisted housing starts in fiscal 1972 for each HUD employee compared to only twelve in fiscal 1976. Senator William Proxmire has remarked that HUD now rivaled the Department of Agriculture in living up to the adage "Give an agency more money and it will produce less."

Despite a moratorium on new housing starts since January, 1973 (with the exception of those already in the pipeline), the agency's total number of employees during each of the fiscal years 1974, 1975, and 1976 remained the same as it was in fiscal 1972. It should also be noted that during this time thirteen community development programs were abolished, consolidated, and transferred to the states and localities to administer. "If recent history shows that more money has produced fewer houses," Proxmire said, "is it not likely that in the future less money would produce more housing? It is my view that we should at least give the concept a try . . . it couldn't be worse than the present situation."

While these programs expend billions of dollars in hard-earned taxes, one cannot overlook the far smaller agencies and programs that, like a horde of Swift's Lilliputians, could bind this nation down to bankruptcy.

The case of one Jubal Hale is the classic example of the bureaucratic microcosms that should be swept from our government. Hale was the $19,000-a-year executive secretary to the Federal Metal and Non-Metalic Safety Board of Review who confessed to a reporter in the summer of 1975 that he and his agency had nothing to do. Indeed, the agency had reviewed nothing for four years, but automatically received its annual appropriation of $60,000. "We have been expecting to be abolished for over two years," the loquacious Hale told a reporter. He recalled that legislation was once introduced to abolish his job, "but nothing happened." He went on to confess that his work days were spent reading and listening to Beethoven on his office stereo. But Hale, like the western hero, has ridden off into the sunset. For Congress, slightly embarrassed by the national press attention paid to Hale's confessions, quietly yet quickly approved legislation to abolish his agency within a matter of weeks. A *Wall Street Journal* editorialist celebrating Hale's departure remarked that "taxpayers can take some satisfaction in the thought that if the job itself wasn't worth the time and space it took up, at least it was occupied by a man of principle. Such a person almost deserves to be paid for doing nothing."

But the fact remains that in our government there are thousands of Jubal Hales and hundreds of agencies like his that have no rational reason for continued existence.

Finding agencies or programs like Hale's is not terribly difficult. Getting rid of them is another matter, as two young and aggressive aides to freshman Senator Patrick Leahy of Vermont discovered.

Assigned by Leahy to devote themselves full-time to uncovering wasteful agencies and programs, the two Vermonters prowled the government's corridors and found numerous programs that should long ago have been ended. One of them—the Federal Fire Council—had done nothing over a seven-year period, yet it received its annual budget of $70,000. Bounced from department to department since its creation in 1936, the council met only once or twice from 1968 to the beginning of 1975. And yet during this period—when the council itself conceded it was "dormant"—a full-time executive director and secretary managed to consume at least $67,000 a year in salaries and office expenses.

Even more amazing is the fact that when Leahy's young aides took their evidence to a Senate appropriations subcommittee and suggested the agency be abolished, the subcommittee balked because it had already completed action on a pending appropriations bill that included the council's money. Staff members argued it would make the subcommittee look bad if they accepted an amendnent at the last minute, knocking out money they should never have approved in the first place. After some pressure, the chairman of the subcommittee, Senator John Pastore of Rhode Island, agreed to accept an amendment cutting off further funds for the agency, with the understanding that Leahy wouldn't embarrass him by making a big speech about it. Such is the receptiveness of Congress to saving the taxpayers' money.

Still, with an annual federal budget boiling over the $400 billion mark it is difficult to expect Congress to be terribly concerned about a $70,000 Federal Fire Council that did nothing for seven years or a $19,000-a-year bureaucrat who spends his time listening to Beethoven. After all, with the government spending $5.8 mililon a year on toilet paper, $1.8 million for rubber bands, and $860,000 for paper clips, what's another $60,000 or $70,000 a year?

Even so, when you add up all these so-called little items, the cost spirals into the billions and adds layers and layers of further bureaucracy.

Each year our government issues millions of publications, guidebooks and how-to pamphlets like *The Pocket Guide to Babysitting* published by HEW and an illustrated booklet issued by the Consumer Information Service that tells housewives how to clean pots and pans.

The National Science Foundation squandered $84,000 on a study of why people fall in love, and then spent another $260,000 to study "passionate love." NSF also teamed up with the National Aeronautics and Space Administration and the Office of Naval Research to spend $500,000 over a seven-year period to determine under what conditions rats, monkeys, and humans bite and clench their jaws.

According to a GAO study, our armed services are spending close to $14 million a year just to maintain some 300 military golf courses in nineteen countries and across the United States.

The National Institute of Child Health and Human Development, a division of the National Institutes of Health, spent over $342,000 to inquire into the sexual habits of university coeds in an effort to find out, among other things, where, when, with whom, and how often they've engaged in sexual activities.

Military surgeons are performing—free of charge—some 800 facelift and breast enlargement operations annually on military wives. Straight-faced military spokesmen say the cosmetic operations help to improve the husbands' morale.

Government vocational education programs are preparing high school and junior college graduates for jobs that do not exist. A GAO investigation found that not only are the jobs not there, but only a third of the students end up working in the skill they learned in school. The study found that in 1972 some 2.5 million high school students, 34 percent of all high school students, were taking home economics courses, which hardly prepares one for future employment. Sixteen percent of the program's 1973 funds, some $63 million, went to fund administrative and other operational costs that did not directly benefit the students. That same year, the program, pictured as an educational disaster by the GAO, consumed $388 million in federal funds and $2.3 billion in state and local funds.

Still another GAO study estimated that about 2170 more employees than necessary were working at Defense Department telecommunications installations around the world. This unneeded manpower costs you $21.7 million a year.

At least 600 government lobbyists, representing virtually every major federal agency, spend their time squeezing bigger budgets out of congressional committees. The Pentagon alone has a fifty-man contingent permanently situated on Capitol Hill. The Environmental Protection Agency employs at least forty-one lobbyists, requiring an annual budget of $944,000. The cost to taxpayers for these gravy-train experts? Fifteen million dollars a year.

Members of Congress are spending almost $46.1 million a year to mail newsletters, questionnaires, government publications, politically self-serving messages, and other so-called official communications to constitutents, all of it paid by taxpayers. Virtually all of this mail is in one way or another connected with the members' desire to win reelection.

The Senate spends $149,000 annually to employ photographers (earning as much as $30,700 a year) to take pictures of senators shaking the hands of constitutents and visiting bigwigs, copies of which are sent out, usually autographed by the senator, to help his reelection. The House also maintains photographers for such uses, but their salaries come from party campaign coffers, not tax revenues.

Government spending has reached such ludicrous heights that we now find ourselves providing novelist Erica Jong with $5000 in tax revenues to help her write her neurotic and sexually explicit book *Fear of Flying*, a literary venture from which she made a small fortune.

For two years the government mailed, at a cost of about $100,000, sex information and condom stamps in unmarked envelopes to lists of teenage boys considered to be sexually active. More than 43,000 boys aged fourteen and up received the stamps, subsidized by the antipoverty progran, but only 254 condom stamps were ever redeemed. It eventually cost taxpayers nearly $400 per package of prophylactics sold through the mail.

The National Institute on Drug Abuse funded a two-year $121,000 study that examined the effects of marijuana on the sexual arousal capacities of young men by allowing college students to smoke pot while watching pornographic movies—at a time when heroin addiction is at an all time high.

About the same time, the Federal Aviation Administration was spending $57,000 on a study entitled "Anthropometry of Airline Stewardesses," which took seventy-nine different body measurements of airline stewardesses from nose to knees. According to the FAA, the study was designed to provide information needed to design seats used by stewardesses on takeoffs and landings. The agency said nothing about the safety-design needs of the passengers' seats. Senator William Proxmire called the study "a bust."

We reach out with ill-conceived programs hoping to help specific blocs of people and continue to expand these programs because these interest groups reap some reward from it, not because the program has proven effective.

For example, House of Representatives investigators found that the Commerce Department's program to promote minority-owned businesses has flopped and shows "little hope for major improvement," but the $50 million-a-year agency goes on.

Officials of the Office of Minority Business Enterprise themselves con-

27

cede that their program is "paralyzed because of internal fighting among minorities," that its policies are under constant political pressures, and that it is often dominated by the business organizations it supports. Moreover, OMBE duplicates the minority business program of the Small Business Administration, and officials and minority businessmen alike say it exists largely to provide employment for the OMBE-funded organizations it supports.

Our GI education benefits program was begun with the best of intentions, but some veterans have apparently ripped off hundreds of millions of dollars from the program. Government investigators found that "students" collected $329.6 million in benefits but did not go to school. And this is just one of countless programs under which checks are mailed out with little or no oversight.

Examples of scandalous misuse and downright squandering of federal money are so numerous that it would require an encyclopedia to detail them all. An investigation of the Federal Reserve System provides the most spectacular example of this kind of waste and wantonness. The investigators found that $389,000 had been spent by Fed banks for cocktail parties and dinners. The Fed's New York bank listed $34,000 for "refreshments" for its officers, staff, and guests. Another $94,000 had been spent on jewelry, watches, lunches, and other items for "employee recognition." Still more thousands of dollars had been spent for holiday parties, with one Fed bank blowing nearly $20,000 on Christmas luncheons and decorations.

The report, prepared by the late House Banking Committee Chairman Wright Patman, listed $762,258 spent in 1974 on 171 persons, corporations, and government agencies for consulting and contract costs, many fees going to former Fed employees and officials. It found $280,000 was spent to move Fed employees from bank to bank, including $14,000 to move one employee and his family only 700 miles. The report said millions more had been spent for an in-house stock investment plan maintained for employees.

The list of waste seems endless. We gave away over $30 billion in revenue-sharing money to 38,000 local and state governments—despite the fact that many localities and states claimed enormous budget surpluses and in spite of a *Washington Post* survey that found there were billions of dollars in federal grants that had never been claimed by local governments. The survey of 1974 and 1975 grants found that more than $5 billion in environmental protection grants, more than $5 billion in Health, Education and Welfare and Department of Agriculture grants, and more than $100 million in community development and highway fund grants went unclaimed.

After spending over $4 billion to fight crime, an Office of Management and Budget memorandum concluded that the Law Enforcement Assistance Administration has wasted our money.

We spent over $205 million for the F-111 jet fighter bombers that the Air Force didn't want. We're spending $354.6 million a year in federal impact aid to education to provide bonus payments to some of the richest school districts in the country. Close to $92 million a year is being spent to continue a Public Health Service hospital system that was established in 1798 to treat victims of plague and other diseases and boasts a vacancy rate of between 30 and 40 percent. Despite high farm income, we're spending $597 million a year on direct payments to farmers. Another half billion dollars a year is spent to subsidize the maritime industry, which after thirty-eight years of handouts still cannot support itself. We find it necessary to spend $5.4 million a year on an Army-Navy-Marine Corps band school near Norfolk, Virginia, to provide a twenty-six-week training course for military musicians.

One top-level bureaucrat, pointing to a fat copy of the federal budget, told a *Los Angeles Times* reporter, ''You better remember, before you talk about waste, that everything in this big book was put there because somebody wanted it, usually somebody powerful. And it's very hard to get anything cut out. Every program gathers supporters the way a ship picks up barnacles.''

The federal government is presently distributing in excess of $56 billion a year to states and localities through more than 1000 aid programs. There is good reason to believe local and state governments could get along with a lot less, say congressional auditors after an eighteen-month study.

As the end of each fiscal year draws near, federal agencies scramble to get rid of their remaining funds. ''The requirements change as June 30 draws closer," said Larry Endy of the General Accounting Office. "Agencies don't like to tell Congress, 'We didn't use all our money.'" Another GAO official said auditors discovered instances in which federal agencies actually telephoned local officials to urge them to apply for funds.

Federal aid of all kinds to local governments has increased sevenfold since 1959. Such aid now comprises 22 percent of all state and local government expenditures. And for some cities and states the search for federal funds has become an industry unto itself. At least eighteen states and some cities operate offices in Washington to "grapple with the maze of federal assistance programs and to reduce the possibility of missing out on available federal assistance," a GAO report said. Some localities pay consultants just to fill out the complex application forms!

For the past four and a half decades we have been on a welfare state treadmill, consuming more and more individual and business earnings for an increasingly vast wasteland of public programs that have either outlived their usefulness or been extravagantly swelled out of proportion to the nation's problems. One need only scan the figures to see where we're heading. In the short span of five years we went from a fiscal 1970 federal budget of $196.6 billion to President Ford's originally proposed fiscal 1976 budget of $358.9 billion—a fantastic 83 percent jump. Every American is going to have to pay for that increase and future increases from his earnings, at the expense of what he would be further providing for himself and his family. And one does not have to be clairvoyant to know that there will be future spending increases as long as Congress continues to act as irresponsibly as it has in the past.

Within Congress there is a seemingly never-ending torrent of spending proposals to take *your* money and spend it on public projects to, supposedly, help people. Whether it's a $100 billion energy development plan, a $110 billion-a-year cradle-to-grave national health insurance program, or a far less ambitious $10 million-a-year National Center for the Prevention and Control of Rape (how rapes can be controlled or even prevented from Washington escapes me), Congress remains an incessant breeding ground for ideas to spend, spend, spend.

But much of this spending and many of these programs have been based on the false assumption that the American people want an ever-expanding government intruding into their lives and dipping into their pocket books. They don't. Surveys show that Americans believe that government has grown too big and too powerful, and that taxes have reached the point of being oppressive.

That message has not been impressed on our lawmakers. Too many of them live in a never-never world of big budgets, pompous proposals, and theoretical problem-solving. They have grown remote from the people they are supposed to represent. Congress in many respects has become a captive to the loudest voices and the most powerful blocs, failing to ascertain what is on the minds of that great majority of nonjoiners and nonprotesters and nonlobbyists. Every indication is that this vast middle ground of Americans is fed up with a system of spending that each year hits them with a bigger bill.

In a recent speech, former HEW Secretary Caspar W. Weinberger warned that

the unplanned, uncoordinated and spasmodic nature of our responses to people's needs—some very real, some only imagined—is quite literally threatening to bring us to national insolvency. If social programs continue growing at their present pace, we could be spending close to half of our whole Gross National Product for domestic social programs alone by the year 2000.

If half the entire GNP should go to pay for domestic social programs, we could not, in all likelihood, maintain our free-enterprise economy. We will then have destroyed the system which has brought more benefits to more people at home and throughout the world than any other system since recorded history began.

The special interests and lawmakers and bureaucrats who want to see the government's role enlarged far beyond its present scope are unconcerned about the ultimate cost to us all. They, like Mayor Wagner in 1965, are not going to let such mundane things as deficits and higher taxes and rising inflation stop their onward rush to bring the hand of government into virtually every human activity. Only the people can bring a halt to this berserk joy ride.

I'm utterly convinced that the trend in spending, borrowing, and taxation can be halted or, at least, substantially slowed. But it will take a concerted, perseverant, overwhelming national drive to enlist every taxpayer to personally demand of his representatives, "Why in heaven's name are we spending money on these programs? Do we really need all these agencies? Do we really want government-financed surveys to find out where, when, and with whom college coeds are having sexual relations? Do we really want more studies such as the Department of Agriculture survey that found out that mothers prefer wrinkle-free childrens clothing? Should budgets continue funding agencies which have had nothing to do for years?"

Eventually, taxpayers themselves must make it abundantly clear to Washington that they have had enough. Perhaps the public attitude that is critically needed today is not terribly unlike the outraged spirit that stirred this nation 200 years ago.

II

Taxes

Is There a Limit?

Year after year debate in Congress over taxes invariably centers around something labeled "reform." Most of the time, however, what emerges is no reform at all. Instead, we are usually presented with a tangle of new tax laws to further complicate an already horribly complex tax system.

For some strange reason the debate over tax reform never includes permanent and generous tax reductions. Such a step is apparently unthinkable.

Members of Congress beat their breasts over the difficulties low and middle income Americans have in coping with the high cost of living, obtaining adequate housing, affording good nutrition, and putting their children through some form of higher education. Lawmakers devise all kinds of intricate schemes to provide new forms of federal aid to help low and lower-middle income groups survive inflation and recession. Seldom, however, does anyone suggest that government could simply abandon many of its domestic spending programs and pass a substantial permanent tax cut. This would be the simplest, cheapest, and most direct aid of all.

Congress did enact a one-year tax cut of relatively minor proportions —only $8 billion—in a desperate attempt to curb a severe recession in early 1975. But the cuts were promulgated on a temporary basis as the hungry jaws of recession snapped at the doors of Congress. The nation was looking to Washington for relief in the midst of severe economic dislocations. The political consequences of inaction were also obvious.

What Congress has not come to grips with is the fundamental question of where to draw the line. How much personal income can government take away from individuals before what is left of our free enterprise system is totally eroded away? Can we go on piling tax upon tax, taxing a person's income up to 70 percent, taxing his savings, taxing his investments, taxing his profit, taxing his estate, taxing the tires on his car, the gas in its tank, and the car itself as if it were some frivolous luxury? Isn't it time we began abolishing many of these ancillary taxes and worked on a comprehensive across-the-board permanent income tax reduction for both individuals and businesses? Isn't it time to begin curbing the trend toward greater and greater expropriation of private income by the state? Isn't it time we realized that it won't be long before continued state expropriation of personal and corporate earnings inflicts irretrievable harm on the productivity, enterprise, and personal incentive that have made America's economy the envy of the world?

As politicians of many persuasions have raised the specters of big oil, "unscrupulous" food retailers, "obscene" profits, and giant multinational corporations bent on "exploitation," they have distracted the attention of the average American taxpayer away from one massive overriding reality: *taxes have outstripped all other cost increases borne by consumers in recent years.*

An annual survey conducted by the Labor Department found that during 1974 taxes took a larger proportional bite out of the American family budget than any other major consumer item. The survey found that the personal income tax bite—state, local and federal—for a lower-level-income family of four earning $9198 a year jumped 25.7 percent from the previous fall. Taxes fo an intermediate-income family of four earning $14,333 per year jumped 25.1 percent. Personal income taxes for a higher-level-income family earning $20,777 per year jumped 26.6 percent.

A report (*Inflation and the Consumer in 1974*) issued by Congress' Joint Economic Committee in February 1975 confirmed the Labor Department's findings for 1974. Even though food prices rose 11.9 percent, housing, 13.5 percent, and transportation, 14.3 percent, personal income and social security taxes rose *twice* as fast.

Senator Hubert Humphrey, the committee chairman, confessed he was amazed to find that "the biggest increases in the middle-income family's budget resulted from higher social security and income tax payments," even though he had no doubt voted for such increases throughout his congressional career.

The study found that for an intermediate-income family earning $14,466, social security taxes rose 21.6 percent in 1974, from $647 in 1973 to $787 in 1974. It found that personal income taxes rose even more for this income level, 26.5 percent. Thus, the intermediate-income family paid $2033 in federal, state, and local income taxes in 1974, compared to $1607 for the previous year—a jump of $426! Meantime, the family's real standard of living remained unchanged.

"Because of our graduated tax rate system," said Humphrey, "taxes are rising faster than any other consumer expenditure in this period of rapid inflation. Not only must workers cope with declining real incomes and the prospect of unemployment, but the percent of their incomes being collected by government is also rising. Most assuredly, this is not the intent of our tax system."

Our tax system may have been developed with the best of intentions, but its actual effect has been to heavily burden individuals desperately trying to cope with the basic problems of providing for their families. And the system is hitting hardest those least able to cope with the heavy and costly hand of government. Thus, the JEC study noted, inflation has

increased the income tax burden on low and middle-income taxpayers more than on wealthy individuals because it has reduced the value of the standard deduction and exemptions and because tax brackets are much narrower at low and middle-income levels. At lower income levels taxpayers are likely to use the standard deduction. While dollar incomes rise, the deduction remains the same, and thus taxable income rises faster than dollar income.

35

At higher income levels, the value of itemized deductions is likely to keep better pace with dollar incomes so that taxable income doesn't rise faster than dollar incomes. Furthermore, families at middle and upper-middle income levels move into higher brackets faster than upper income families during inflationary periods.

Thus, a family with a joint income of $32,000 in 1973 would have been taxed at a 42 percent marginal rate, the report said. But if the family's dollar income rose by the 12 percent inflation rate in 1974, it would have been shoved into the 45 percent tax bracket. However, a family earning $50,000 in 1973 could have increased its income by 12 percent or more in 1974 and still remained in the same tax bracket. "Thus, inflation makes the tax system less progressive," the report said.

Here's an illustration from the JEC report that shows how inflation reduces the real value of the personal exemption and the standard deduction, hurting low and moderate income groups most:

An average four-person family with an income of $13,000 in 1973 took the standard deduction and paid $1391 in federal income taxes. Its disposable, after-tax income was $11,609. Let us assume that this family's income rose 8 per cent in 1974 (per capita personal income rose 8.3 per cent from third quarter 1973 to third quarter 1974) to $14,040. This family would be liable for $1609 in federal income taxes and its after-tax income would be $12,431. This means that family's after-tax income in dollar terms has risen by 7 per cent. The higher taxes which resulted from the diminished value of the standard deduction and the exemption actually increased the tax burden on this family from 10.7 per cent of income to 11.5 per cent.

In real terms, of course, this family's real after-tax income has fallen as a result of higher taxes and inflation. Measured in 1973 dollars, its 1974 disposable income of $12,431 is actually worth only $10,939. Therefore, even though the family's income rose by 8 per cent during 1974, its purchasing power has dropped 6 per cent.

Even if this family's income had risen by the rate of inflation, 12 per cent, its after-tax purchasing power would have declined 3 per cent from 1973 to 1974.

So, not only does government fuel inflation with its vast and undisciplined spending, but it also inflicts an invidious tax system that allows the inflation created by government to further punish the average taxpayer struggling to cope with the high cost of living.

In addition to tax reductions for individuals, Congress included in its 1975 temporary tax cut package between $100 and $200 in individual tax rebates. In light of the tax increases that struck middle-income families during 1974, the rebates were rather meager. Humphrey's report showed that a family of four who earned $14,466 paid an additional $140 in social security taxes and $426 extra in federal, state, and local income taxes in 1974. The family's rebate was about a quarter of what it paid in additional taxes. The family that earned $13,000 in 1973 and $14,040 in 1974 received a rebate of $150, or about one-tenth of the $1492 it had, in effect, lost in real disposable income as a result of inflation. "Government giveth and government taketh away," remarked columnist George Will at the time, "and it does a lot more of the latter than of the former. So Humphrey should not be amazed if the public, once it has those rebate checks in hand, still feels filleted."

A third and more extensive study has confirmed what is happening to taxes in this country. An analysis by the Conference Board, an independent business economic research group, found that over the past six years taxes have risen more rapidly than any other item in the American family's budget. The analysis showed that both income and social security taxes have skyrocketed nearly 65 percent since 1967. During the same period, the cost of food, housing, clothing, and other goods and services rose "only" 35 percent.

All one has to do is look at the cumulative tax totals on the last paycheck stub of the year to truly comprehend what is going on in Washington today. The withholding and other tax figures on a fellow journalist's last paycheck statement for 1974 provide a good example of the entire tragic picture. Married, with one child, this reporter had a gross income for the year of $15,707. His federal withholding tax (which he earned and his employer paid—not to him but to the federal government) totaled $2451. His total social security payments were $772. His state withholding was $596. The grand total taxed from his earnings was the incredible sum of $3819, over 24 percent of his earnings! I submit that for an individual supporting a wife and child on a little over $15,000 a year, this is an unconscionable sum to take from his earnings. And the above figures do *not* include the tax on his modest savings, the state sales tax, a myriad of federal excise and sales taxes he must pay throughout the year, other state and local fees and taxes, plus the increased cost of everything he purchases and consumes because of higher prices passed on to him through business taxes—not to mention government-created inflation.

Americans are being virtually smothered in taxes. As a country lawyer once cracked, "It would be criminal if it were not legal."

President Ford's October, 1975, proposal for nearly $28 billion in permanent tax cuts for individuals and businesses was a step in the right direction, but I don't think even Ford's cuts went far enough. They would have still required a family of four with gross earnings of $15,000 to pay $1325 in federal income taxes, not to mention social security and state taxes and all the other governmental levies on income. They would have still required a similar family with a $7000 income to pay $60 in federal income taxes. (Such a family paid $402 in taxes in 1974 and—under Congress' temporary tax cuts—paid $186 in taxes in 1975.) Anyone with two children to care for on an income that isn't too far above the poverty level shouldn't have to pay any income taxes. I find it incredible that under our so-called progressive federal tax structure a family of four with a gross income of $5000 was forced to pay $98 in taxes in 1974. Mercifully, under the temporary 1975 cuts they paid nothing.

President Ford tied his sweeping tax cut proposal to a call for an identical $28 billion cut in spending. This would have gone a long way toward reversing the seemingly unending trend in heavier taxes, deeper deficits, and bulging budgets. But Congress—unable to break its addiction to big spending—wanted no part of the $395 billion spending ceiling for fiscal year 1977 that Ford linked to his tax package. "Irresponsible," snapped Representative Al Ulman, chairman of the House Ways and Means Committee. "No way," declared Senator Russell Long, chairman of the Senate Finance Committee.

Ford's proposal would have permanently cut income taxes to $20.7 billion below the 1974 tax levels for individuals and $7 billion for businesses. The cuts would have been about $11 billion below the temporary 1975 antirecession cuts. The proposal would have increased personal exemptions from $750 to $1000; provided a flat $2500 standard deduction on joint returns, regardless of income; provided lower tax rates for those in the low and moderate income brackets; reduced tax rates on the first $50,000 of corporate profits and reduced the maximum corporate tax rate from 48 percent to 46 percent; permanently increased the investment tax-credit to 10 percent; and provided special tax incentives to electric utilities and stockholders to encourage conversion from oil to other sources of energy.

The important difference between Congress' tax cut and Ford's proposal was, of course, that the president wanted a parallel cut in spending to match lost revenue. With spending continuing to rise and a $74–80 billion plus deficit facing Washington in fiscal 1976, that money had to be made up somewhere. In truth, the sum would be borrowed and the debt would be paid eventually by taxpayers one way or another. Tax cuts without spending reductions are as phony as a $3 bill. They merely postpone bills which eventually must come due.

Those Americans who work hard, perhaps at times harder than they have to, to provide their families and themselves with the basic comforts and advantages of life, know the reward that hard work can bring, not only materially but also the inner satisfaction that that extra effort helped to obtain something more for their family's financial security. Our society is built upon this fiber of personal incentive that threads its way through our economic structure. If you work hard, perhaps harder than the next guy, you can reap the fruits of your labor and be proud of your accomplishments whatever their level.

But, as we have seen, our tax system penalizes anyone who ventures forth to earn more, shoving him into a more onerous tax bracket where a larger percentage of his earnings are taken. How many times have you heard a blue collar worker complain after having worked overtime at time-and-a-half that it wasn't worth it because so much of his additional earnings were consumed by taxes? Remember our beleaguered middle income reporter? His situation was made even worse when, after earning an additional $2000 through some extra writing, Uncle Sam demanded another $400 in income taxes on top of the $3800 he had already paid.

Despite continuation of the 1975 tax cuts, passed primarily to revive a sluggish economy (not to provide relief for the American taxpayer), taxes

39

are still unnecessarily high. And when the economy is in full bloom again, and the accumulated deficits caused by the temporary cuts must be paid, the suspended taxes will no doubt be reimposed, perhaps at even higher levels.

But why must it necessarily be that way? Instead of taking more money from the pockets of Americans so that part of it can be returned to them in the form of multitudinous aid programs, rebates, and other schemes, why not leave the bulk of America's income with those who earned it so they can provide for more of their own needs and wants? It is an old fashioned idea, but one that is still viable, and needed now more than ever before.

III

The Economy

Is Private Enterprise Dying?

America's economy is slowly and systematically being killed by government.

The average man in the street doesn't understand this because he has believed politicians who have told him that business is to blame for all his woes, that greedy, unscrupulous businessmen are making money hand over fist at his expense by charging unconscionable prices and making "obscene" profits. When government policies fail, which is often, politicians blame business, Washington's convenient whipping boy for decades.

A long time ago an American president declared that the business of America is business. Since that time Americans have been led to believe that business is somehow an alien presence in our society, that it must be interrogated, regulated, fought, and even suppressed. Listening to members of Congress righteously excoriate the business community while glorifying themselves for their (failing) public programs, one gets the distinct impression that Congress believes the economy revolves around government, a potentially errant satellite that must be carefully controlled lest it swerve out of orbit. Who do the politicians think provides the jobs in this country? From where do they think incomes are derived? Who do they think develops the machinery, technology, research, productivity, and economic drive that fuel this nation's capacities and have made it the wealthiest and most influential country on the face of the earth? Who do they think will *really* deal with unemployment? Alas, there are times when Congress appears to think that America's business is government.

In large measure, the problem results from some gross distortions in the public's perception of business. A nationwide survey once asked Americans to guess what the average profits were for American corporations. Most people believed profits averaged around 33 percent a year. Actually, the average corporation earns about 5 percent profit annually after taxes, which isn't terribly high, considering that from this shareholders must be paid a reasonable return on their investment. The balance, if there is any, goes for repairs and plant modernization.

Many in Washington have also created the impression that the business conmunity is not paying its share of the nation's tax burden. Business paid 23 percent of all federal taxes in 1960. Today it pays 17 percent. The reason for the reduced percentage is something most Americans have not been told and fewer still would probably believe. For the fact is that the percentage of national income represented by business profits has been shrinking. Business profits in 1965 made up 6.8 percent of all national income. That share dropped to 3.8 percent in 1969 and to 3.3 percent in 1973.

But how is it possible, if business profits comprise 3 percent of all national income, for business to provide 17 percent of all federal tax revenues? The answer in part is that business is very heavily taxed in this country, far more heavily than in most other countries, even Sweden with its vast welfare state. In fact, the basic corporate tax rate, state and federal, is now close to 60 percent.

Such draconian taxation is slowly breaking the back of business and strongly discouraging the kind of capital formation that is desperately needed if we are to forestall an anticipated capital shortfall by 1985 of some $400 million a day. The New York Stock Exchange has estimated a "gap" for all domestic borrowers over the next decade of around $650 billion.

Incredible as it may see, the United States' industrial plant today is older than either Europe's or Japan's. A Treasury Department study found that America is investing much less of its national output in productive capacity (only 13.6 percent) than Japan (29 percent), West Germany (20 percent), France (18.2 percent), or Canada (17.4 percent).

It doesn't take an advanced degree in economics to see that the failure to close the capital investment gap will result in continued and even higher unemployment and a higher rate of inflation in the years ahead. Credit is the life blood of American business, and when government preempts its supply through intense borrowing to finance deficit spending that in turn drives up interest rates to the detriment of every businessman and every consumer, the economy gets into trouble. Clearly, heavy federal borrowing from the private money markets—not to mention the additional borrowing demands by agencies whose operations are not included in the federal budget—(over $1.5 billion a week!) is preventing a healthy economic recovery and fanning the fires of inflation.

A government that racks up a $44 billion deficit in fiscal 1975 and then goes on to charge up a $75–80 billion deficit in fiscal 1976 must get that money somewhere. Through notes and bonds offered at interest rates of from 7 to 8 percent and higher, that money is being taken from our economy. The credit available to the business community is thus restricted, heavier federal spending naturally forces up demand, and interest rates for the average businessman rise. So, to the detriment of every consumer, do prices.

As America's capital increasingly flows into Washington, business' capital-starvation problems worsen. A study entitled *Capital Needs In the Seventies* by the liberal Brookings Institution acknowledges that capital formation will be a problen in the years ahead if the economy is to develop new sources of energy and create needed jobs. The study concludes that there will be enough capital investment through the rest of the 1970s, but "just barely." It warns that it will take prudent fiscal management by government to avoid a crunch in the capital market or a renewed inflationary spiral. But, surprisingly, the study says a government budget *surplus* will be required to finance needed investment. The study suggests that the government must run an average surplus of $11.5 billion a year between 1974 and 1980. Figuring the 1974–76 federal deficits at around $150 billion, the Brookings analysis would require surpluses of around $70 billion each year between fiscal 1977 and fiscal 1980. Such a proposition, observed the *Wall Street Journal,* "can only be described as laughable."

Thus, while some liberals are belatedly acknowledging the problem of capital formation, they do not appear willing to take the hard steps needed to achieve a prudent solution. Such a solution certainly requires a substantial reduction in taxes on capital, more realistic depreciation allowances, tax preferences when corporate earnings are plowed back into business, easing capital gains taxes, and incentives to encourage personal savings.

It is in this last area of savings and the federal government's heavy borrowing policies that We find one of the most critical aspects of the economy's inability to fully recover. Attractively high interest rates on federal notes are siphoning off deposits from America's savings and loan institutions, to the severe detriment of the private lending markets, particularly the mortgage and housing industries, who depend on these banking institutions. Obviously, when one can get 8.44 percent on a two-year note from the Treasury, there's little incentive to put one's savings into a savings and loan institution at about 7 percent. This has had a crushing effect on the nation's housing industry, which in turn adversely affects related industries.

The shift in funds by investors from savings institutions into higher-yield investments is called disintermediation. The experts in the field know what its effect is on housing. George Hanc, chief economist for the National Association of Mutual Savings Banks, said, "It doesn't take Sherlock Holmes to know that a basic factor has been the rise in open-market yields," with the competition coming "mainly from Treasury financings." Henry Kaufman, chief economist for Salomon Brothers, the brokerage and investment firm, said he saw no letup in the outflow of savings as long as the government continued to borrow heavily to fund its growing debt. "The current interest rate structure is very unfavorable for housing activity, and there is no way housing can get a second-stage lift unless [federal lending] interest rates come down."

Yet amidst this sad state of affairs members of Congress were proposing multi-billion-dollar housing programs that would have required higher deficits and more borrowing and still more disintermediation, which would

44

virtually cut the heart out of the housing industry. Few suggested that the government should reduce spending, slash borrowing, and allow the savings and loan and other banking institutions to accumulate deposits that would help the housing industry get back on its feet. For a while in early 1975 Congress considered legislation that would have exempted from taxation the first $500 in interest earned from savings. It was a sensible incentive for increasing the inflow of savings deposits, but Congress couldn't bear the thought of losing tax revenue from the small- and average-income saver.

While it is clear that heavy federal borrowing almost always leads to higher interest rates, the argument is inevitably made by such liberal economic writers as the *Washington Post*'s Hobart Rowen that interest rates can be brought down if the Federal Reserve Board would only expand the money supply. Economist Arthur M. Okun, among others, has made similar pleas for a more liberal Fed monetary policy.

Allowing the money supply "to grow at a comparably generous rate," as Rowen would have the Fed do, would only further ignite inflationary pressures. This of course is a predictable result, as Ezra Solomon, professor of economics at Stanford University and a member of the Council of Economic Advisers, persuasively outlines in his book *The Anxious Economy*. While Solomon lists a number of factors leading to inflation, he argues that the primary cause is excess demand triggered by the over-creation of money. For anyone who doubts that cause and effect relationship, Solomon reveals that from 1955 to 1964, when the money supply was expanded at 2 percent a year, prices rose 1.6 percent a year (remember those good old days?). But when the growth of the money supply was rapidly accelerated between 1965 and 1970, and boosted still further between 1970 and 1974, prices took off, too.

Unfortunately, too many influential Democrats in Congress agree with Rowen and have religiously urged Federal Reserve Board Chairman Arthur Burns to heat up the economy by pumping up the money supply. Apparently, none of them is willing to admit that the government's credit demands in the private market have anything to do with higher interest rates, nor are they willing to concede that by artificially increasing the money supply a bad situation is made worse.

45

Interest rates rose throughout 1975 as the Treasury dipped deeply into the money markets. The same was true in previous years. In a letter to the *Washington Post,* Senator James Buckley of New York provided a clear picture of what happens when this sort of policy is pursued:

> When interest rates began to move up in 1972, what is it the Federal Reserve did? It did exactly what Messrs. Rowen and Okun would have them do now: increase the rate of growth of the money supply. For what purpose? To keep interest rates lower than credit market forces would otherwise dictate. What was the result? Interest rates soared. Why? Because rational lenders and borrowers understood that rapid money supply growth was significantly accelerating the inflation spiral. Under these circumstances, lenders did not want to extend credit at rates that are lower than the anticipated rate of inflation. By the same token, the expectation of soaring inflation causes borrowers to boost the amount they are willing to pay for long term credit.

Senator Buckley concludes that "an attempt to push into the economy a supply of money which the economy is unable to accommodate is to lay the seeds of a new inflation, the anticipation of which pushes interest rates higher than they would otherwise be. . . . Rowen has failed to observe that our present recession is to a significant extent traceable to the inflation of 1973–74. And the inflation is traceable in substantial part to an extraordinary expansionary monetary policy beginning in 1970."

Interestingly enough, at the time Rowen was suggesting increased growth of the money supply as a means of achieving a quick economic recovery, Fed policies were anything but restrictive. In fact, the money supply had been growing at an annual rate of almost 10 percent since March, 1975.

Any artificial boost in the money supply only serves to dilute the dollars already in circulation, diminishing their purchasing power. Heavy federal borrowing during a recessionary period plus an artificial increase in the money supply only forestalls economic recovery, fans inflation, raises interest rates, and ultimately leads to another recession.

Another major area of concern in our economy is the smothering embrace of government regulation and its adverse effect on business growth, productivity, and consumer prices. An incredible multitude of new laws and regulations forced businessmen to devote 20 percent more of their time in 1975 than in the previous year to filling out the 114 million or more different forms that Washington demands of them. Each year, as Congress passes new laws requiring new government regulations, the amount of time businesses must spend filling out forms increases. A new industry of specialists has come into being to advise and assist businessmen in complying with all the forms and records required by Washington's myriad bureaucracies.

For example, the Federal Trade Commission has developed one new form that asks companies to report sales by product lines. A Virginia direct-mail businessman complained that for a relatively small mailing for the Civil Service Commission he was presented with almost forty pages of instructions and federal prerequisites just to bid on the job. He turned it down because his cost just to comply with the forms "wasn't worth it. We would have had to hire an attorney to decipher all this gobbledygook," he told me.

A Labor Department survey of how small firms try to cope with government regulation displays in vivid and often tragic detail the extent to which federal forms are overwhelming and embittering the average businessman and causing him to feel that the government "is out to get me." Most businessmen cannot begin to understand all that is required of them. Members of Congress—who write the laws—don't even know. One businessman said, "There is no way you can keep up with all the regulations and run a business at the same time," adding that there are "bound to be some laws that we're not following because they may not have filtered down to this level." The president of a fifty-year-old family-owned metal foundry said, "I feel like an awful lot of people do. We need less meddling from the government. We should get back to the good old solid ways of supply amd demand and let business regulate itself. Competition will make necessary a lot of the improvements that are required, without being regulated by Washington."

The head of a small oil firm with 200 employees told the Labor Department investigators he had to "rely on outside sources of information to clarify [his] legal obligations" in order to comply with the laws. He

47

estimated that it would cost $100,000 a year if his company did the job in-house. "A businessman must have an interpreter of regulations," he said.

Ultimately, businessmen have come to fear the specter of federal intrusion. An official of a machine parts company said, "Most businessmen are scared to death of coming to the attention of the government. There's a fear that if you ask a question, you're implying that you're doing something wrong and asking for an investigator to come in. You just don't want your name on a list." He said his company spent between $12,000 and $15,000 a year to answer government questions and surveys. And if the feeling is spreading that government would just as soon punish businessmen as help them, it's not surprising. The official recalled the comment of a federal compliance officer concerning a discrimination suit that had been filed against another firm: "If you go bankrupt, you deserve it. You're going to pay for the sins of discrimination you've committed over the years." Is it any wonder that small businessmen feel they "are being hemmed in on all sides by big labor, big management, and big government"?

And who pays for all the paperwork, regulations, compliance procedures, surveys, studies, and God-knows-what? Obviously, the American consumer does, for every last bit of it. The full cost of this regulatory nightmare has been stunningly revealed by economist Murray L. Weidenbaum in his American Enterprise Institute study *Government-Mandated Price Increases*. Here are some examples of Weidenbaum's findings: Government safety and environmental requirements added about $320 to the cost of the average 1974 automobile. By prohibiting free interstate competition among rail, bus, and trucking industries, the Interstate Commerce Commission is costing consumers between $5 billion and $10 billion a year in higher prices for almost everything they buy. The Civil Aeronautics Board similarly prohibits free-market competition among interstate airlines. For example, Trans World Airlines, because it operates interstate, must charge a fixed fare for a Los Angeles to San Francisco ticket that is 40 percent higher than the charge for the same trip by Pacific Southwest Airlines, an airline that flies only within California and is thus free of CAB regulation. The Occupational Safety and Health Administration, the Federal Power Commission, the Federal Communications Commission, the

Securities and Exchange Commission, the Environmental Protection Agency, the Consumer Product Safety Commission and a mountain of other agencies impose numerous hidden costs on our economy. All are borne by *you*, the consumer, through higher prices.

Burdened with excessive government controls, confronted with government-subsidized competitors, and drained by a multitude of federal, state, and local taxes (one study found over 100 different taxes affecting the price of a loaf of bread), America's economy is struggling for survival. The outlook is bleak, especially when one considers the results of a Commerce Department survey showing that 56 percent of the American people want more government regulation, while 20 percent say they want more controls over big business in particular. Twenty-four percent say they do not know what "private enterprise" means.

What is killing free enterprise? Government regulation, unrelenting taxation, and a myriad of anticompetitive subsidies.

Government shovels billions in subsidies to our highways, airlines, and trucking industries, drowns the railroads in a network of regulations, and later wonders why the rails have tumbled into an abyss of bankruptcy and decay. Then it comes forward with multi-billion-dollar programs to rescue the Northeast railroads from the consequences of these disastrous policies.

Frequently, the federal government subsidizes businessmen seeking to "compete" with other small businessmen who must operate without government aid and with loans at far higher interest rates. I recall, for instance, the phone call of a distraught small businessman from Roanoke, Virginia, who found one day after years of building up his business in the corrugated cardboard industry that he was confronted by a competitor in his area—a situation he was more than willing to face in a free competitive climate. But this competitor came into the area with a $500,000 low-interest federal loan that gave him a considerable competitive edge. "It's not fair," the businessman complained. "I started my business with a few thousand dollars in personal savings. He gets a government loan. Is this the way our government helps small businessmen?"

There are some basic economic misconceptions that must be cleared up if our economy is going to be turned around. First, *profit* is not a dirty word. Profit is the critical margin of money business makes after expenses

49

and taxes that makes possible wage increases, improved worker benefits, and plant expansion and development to create more jobs. Profit pushes our economy upward. Although surveys show that the public believes the average manufacturer makes a profit of twenty-eight cents out of every dollar he takes in, the real figure is about four cents after taxes. The giant supermarket chains make only about a penny and a half out of every dollar in sales. For all nonfinancial corporations, including manufacturers and others, after-tax profits amount to about 2.3 cents. On investments, profits after taxes average 11 percent—and they have been going down since World War II.

Second, government accomplishes very little by taxing its citizens more so that the revenues can be placed into the economy through various economic development and business assistance programs. Remember, *government can put into the economy only what it first takes out.*

Third, too many business sectors have come to depend upon government subsidies and protective regulation. They have become used to the federal dole and find the habit difficult to break. Congressional studies show, for example, that there is no longer any compelling need for local air subsidies. A number of agricultural industries could pay the cost of their commodity inspections, classifications, and other services. The big trucking firms and the giant airlines like existing regulations because the resulting cartels keep out competition. Both the subsidies and the cartels should be ended.

Fourth, government must drop the notion that it is bad to allow a major corporation to go out of business. Failing companies should be allowed to die with dignity. That is the law of the market place. The weak, inefficient, mismanaged, or outmoded should not, and cannot, survive in a free competitive economy. By artificially propping up such companies with federal aid, government only worsens the dislocations in the affected segment of the economy and prolongs the time when new and more viable firms or industries can move in to "claim the territory."

Fifth, America's small businesses are not going to be saved in our giant-oriented economy without the help of major tax reductions. Our antiquated business income tax structure dates back to 1950. It has become so archaic and so regressive that the effective tax rates for a medium-sized business may be twice as high as the rates paid by giant corporations.

Finally, it must be conceded that business is in part to blame for much of its own predicament. Too often business has sought favors from government, cozied up to its regulatory agencies, lobbied for every subsidy it could get, and almost silently accepted the derogations of Washington officialdom. "Unfortunately," wrote columnist Kevin Phillips, "the boardroom bureaucrats who run American business don't have the moxie to confront this issue head-on. Too many of them are content to live on past glory and past profits, using up the accumulated economic muscle of bygone decades." The big businessmen who are dragged before congressional committees to apologize for trying to make a profit had better shift into an offensive position soon—before it is too late. They have little to apologize for.

Treasury Secretary Simon has correctly observed that government "has grown swollen and fat" while the business sector "has grown weak from undernourishment." What Congress and the regulators must eventually come to understand is that continually rising deficits and heavy federal spending only fuel the nation's demands for goods and services, doing little to improve America's capacity to produce. Only by freeing business of unnecessary federal regulation and encroachment, by ending the adversary relationship that has developed between government and business, and by gradually reducing the incentive-sapping taxation that is punishing every business—and ultimately every consumer—can we improve America's productivity and the earnings of all its citizens.

IV

Welfare

How Much Can We Afford?

After three and a half decades of a rapidly expanding welfare state, the view that government is spending more than it—than *we*—can afford is gaining widespread acceptance. Criticism of state and national welfare programs is no longer the sole preserve of America's conservatives. Most liberals and conservatives now agree that America's existing welfare program is a mess.

Senator Abraham A. Ribicoff of Connecticut, after being intimately involved in state and national welfare programs, both as a governor and as a HEW secretary under President Kennedy, admitted in a little-noticed confessional that after a decade of spending "it is clear that our antipoverty efforts failed."

In his book *America Can Make It!*, Ribicoff stunningly exposed what really happened under President Johnson's Great Society antipoverty program, the Office of Economic Opportunity:

> The middlemen—not the poor—are moving forward in the economy as a result of the war on poverty. Former OEO Director Donald Rumsfeld has

53

estimated that 2 million people are employed by federal, state and local governments to administer programs to aid the 26 million poor. In addition, there are scores of former antipoverty officials, and hundreds of private management consulting firms they go to work for [who] are living off the poor. There is big money in poverty—big money for everybody, that is, except the poor. Since OEO was established six years ago, for example, some $600 million has been spent on contracts to private consulting firms for consultation, evaluation, technical assistance and support, including 44 evaluations of Project Head Start.

In 1970, OEO was paying on 128 consultation, evaluation, technical assistance and support contracts worth $56.7 million. Thirty-two of these contracts worth $11.5 million were held by sixteen companies which had thirty-five former OEO officials working for them. At least 254 firms were found to have received $100,000 or more in OEO contracts. Of these, 127 have headquarters or branch offices in the Washington, D.C., area.

As one poverty worker confided in me, "I have no illusions, senator. I'm in poverty for the money." This young man was making more money than he had ever made in his life.

As Ribicoff vividly detailed, hundreds of millions of dollars, perhaps even billions, never got down to the poor. The bulk of the money went to support an army of so-called poverty workers and a library full of consultant studies conducted by research outfits making a fast buck off the fashionable political issue of the day. Yesterday it was poverty. Today it may be energy.

But President Johnson elevated the politics of poverty to a high art in his day, making the ultimate campaign promise: government would abolish poverty by spending tax money on the poor. It was a naive gesture from the beginning, but the fabled 89th Congress was ready to pass virtually any kind of social legislation that accomplished at least two things: spent money and created new federal bureaucracies. Johnson's antipoverty measures did both on the grand scale in which he so often fantasized. Ten years later, Ribicoff, one of the program's most ardent supporters, has given us the results: after more than $10 billion, total and undeniable failure.

One need merely gaze across a vast wasteland of social programs to see failure after failure. The food stamp program is a case in point. It has been

54

allowed to grow all out of proportion to both the need for it and the ability of taxpayers to support it. Begun as a pilot program in 1961, its cost has grown from $3.8 million in the first year to more than $6 billion a year —amounting to about two-thirds of the Department of Agriculture's total budget. Some 1600 federal employees administer the program, which in 1975 was providing food stamps for almost one out of every eleven Americans, more than 19 million people. It costs taxpayers more than one dollar and nine cents to provide a dollar's worth of food stamps, which, incidentally, have a value to recipients of eighty-three cents.

If the program is on a grand scale, so are the errors and abuse. A Treasury Department study showed that more than 9 million food stamp recipients were not eligible to receive them or received too many or too few. The study said that one out of every six persons on food stamps had an annual income of $12,000 or was otherwise ineligible for the program. About two out of five food stamp users got too many. As a result of these abuses, one out of eight eligible persons got less than they were entitled to. A Treasury official called the abuses "incredible," and said the program's loose administration at the state level was costing taxpayers between $500 million and $1 billion a year.

The *Report of the Findings on Food Stamp Efficiency,* a recent (September, 1975) Senate Government Operations Committee study, declared that the program's costs

due to inefficiency and errors had risen alarmingly. USDA figures show an overall nationwide error rate for program requirement areas of 18 per cent for the six-month period ending June 30, 1974. Further statistics related that for the same period 11 per cent of eligible recipients were overcharged for their stamps and 26 per cent were undercharged. A total of 7 per cent of all recipients were found to have been improperly denied benefits. Clearly the waste and red tape spawned by inefficient administration not only detracts from the program in the eyes of the taxpayer, but, more importantly, the big loser is the recipient.

A quick look at the program shows that Congress legislatively mandates the program, Agriculture (USDA) sets the regulations to conform to the legislative intent, and the actual implementation of the program is left in the hands of state welfare agencies to carry the program out on the local level.

State agencies many times are left alone to interpret, digest, and enforce a never-ending stream of regulations and court decisions.

The end result is that the Food Stamp Program is plagued by fragmented and inconsistent regulations that cause program duplication and complexity. The duplication contributes to waste and an error-ridden program that neither helps the recipient nor is conducive to efficient administration.

Carl B. Williams, deputy U.S. commissioner of welfare, told *U.S. News and World Report* that "as it now stands, the food stamp system is in such a mess that the government has practically abdicated its responsibility for seeing that money gets to people who really need it. In effect, billions of dollars are being given away with virtually no controls." Moreover, an unknown number of food stanps are being lost to counterfeiting and black-market racketeering. Williams described it this way: "If a person gets $100 in food stamps that he wants to spend on rent or booze, he just sells them to a black marketeer for, say, $80. The middleman then sells them for $90 to a crooked grocer, who gets the full $100 from the government." Declared Williams, "I'm convinced that taxpayers, through food stamps, are innocently supporting an enormous amount of illegal 'street business'—from drugs to crap games and prostitution."

Early in 1975 President Ford submitted proposed legislation that would have required program participants to pay a small additional share of their total income for food stamps. The legislation would have halted much of the abuse by tightening eligibility requirements and saved taxpayers up to $1 billion in fiscal year 1976. Congress rejected it.

What mystifies most Americans is how government welfare programs can begin so modestly and then become totally uncontrollable—a bottomless pit for both the needy and the greedy. The government's budget bureau said in its fiscal 1975 budget proposals that 73.5 percent of all spending in that year would be "relatively uncontrollable." Is it possible that Congress approves programs over which no one in the government can exert any control? Not exactly. What the bureaucrats mean by uncontrollable is that the government's obligations have been fixed by Congress. In the case of the food stamp stampede, Congress left the program's budget open-ended—in other words, it gave the bureaucrats a blank check. In the sense that Congress was willing to spend whatever the traffic would bear, the

56

program was practically "uncontrollable." If everyone eligible under the program's broad criteria were to sign up for its benefits, an estimated 40–60 million Americans would be on food stamps.

But, of course, there is no such thing as uncontrolled federal spending. It is uncontrolled only insofar as the Office of Management and Budget cannot change the laws as fixed by Congress. The words that make up the laws or programs are just that, words. Words that can be changed by Congress. There is nothing uncontrollable about an act of Congress, difficult as that may be for some to believe. Each and every law can be repealed or modified by a simple majority of the House and Senate. That Congress chooses to enact loosely written programs with no spending ceilings shows its utter disregard for the peoples' tax dollars.

A brilliant case study (*Uncontrollable Spending for Social Services Grants*) of such open-ended welfare spending was made in 1975 by Brookings Institution analyst Martha Derthick. The study concerned grants-in-aid for various social services programs begun in 1962. The program, to fund a variety of state programs for the poor, sick, and handicapped, was open-ended. Under it, spending skyrocketed from $354 million in fiscal 1969 to $1.69 billion in fiscal 1972—a fourfold increase. At the time, House Ways and Means Committee Chairman Wilbur Mills denounced the progran as "the worst loophole that has ever been written into the law on the financing of government."

What had occurred was that Congress had written a spending program with language and purposes so vague and ill-defined that it could be used to fund virtually any social program. Once the states had discovered its possibilities, it was like a one-day half-price closeout sale. Illinois virtually covered its estimated 1972 budget deficit with funds from the program. State governors got together to discuss how they could exploit this new-found pipeline to Washington's fabled bottomless pit, estimating they would seek $4.7 billion in fiscal 1973 alone.

In the end, Congress supposedly closed the loophole, imposing a $2.5 billion a year ceiling on the grants and limiting each state's share to its percentage of the national population. But insofar as Congress set no specific limit on what may be spent in any given fiscal year, the program continues in fact to be open-ended.

Congress has not learned its lesson, as open-ended social services and sd stamp programs are proving. A host of other so-called uncontrollable programs, such as welfare assistance, Medicaid, Social Security, Medicare, Supplemental Security Income, and student loans, fall into the same category. Incredibly, 80 percent of HEW's appropriations—which account for more than one-third of the government's total budget—are presently open-ended.

We are careening out of control on a welfare state rollercoaster, and Congress doesn't appear to be interested in applying the brakes. Total welfare payments recently jumped by 19.9 percent, from $18.8 billion in 1974 to almost $22.6 billion by mid-1975. All twenty-six welfare indicators went up in 1975, including money payments to recipients, numbers of children and adults on welfare, emergency aid to families, and medical care benefits. In fact, HEW's total welfare costs rose in June, 1975, despite a decline in the number of persons on welfare. There are over 11.3 million individuals among some 3.4 million families presently receiving some form of federal welfare.

Administrations come and go expressing the best of intentions to curb uncontrolled welfare spending, but clearly more is needed than good intentions. Former HEW Secretary Caspar Weinberger displayed all the correct rhetoric about curbing welfare costs, but under him HEW's spending jumped an estimated 18 percent in fiscal 1975, as compared to a 13 percent increase in 1968 under the Johnson Administration. To Weinberger's credit, however, he did reduce the national error rate in welfare payments. But errors in overpayments, underpayments, or payments to ineligible welfare recipients still remain much higher than the goals the agency set for itself for June, 1975.

Despite all the conservative rhetoric of the Nixon and Ford administrations, spending on social welfare programs has skyrocketed. Federal outlays for welfare have leaped 300 percent in the past six years. They jumped 178 percent for Medicare and Medicaid payments, which were expected to shoot from $25 billion in 1975 to $52 billion by 1980. Jonathan Spivak, the *Wall Street Journal*'s HEW reporter, observed that as of 1973 social welfare spending at all levels of the federal government had exceeded $1000 per capita, or more than the infamous $1000 checks Senator George McGovern promised in his 1972 presidential campaign.

Social Security retirement payments contribute more than any other single factor to this alarming rise in welfare spending. Benefits have risen by nearly 74 percent since 1968, more than twice the cost-of-living increase. In 1975 Social Security outlays were an estimated $75 billion, more than the entire 1957 federal budget.

With almost 30 million Americans receiving Social Security payments, the system is now running an annual deficit of $2.5 billion. This has occurred despite sharp rises in Social Security taxes in the last six years. In 1970 the maximum combined employer-employee tax was $748.80 per year. By 1976 it had gone over $1649.70 per year. It is estimated that an increase in the payroll tax of from 10 percent to 25 percent will be needed from now to the year 2000 to avoid a reduction in benefits. At the end of 1975 the Social Security trust fund totaled $43.4 billion, or 66 percent of a year's benefit payments. By 1980 the reserves are expected to drop to a low of $800 million, or enough to pay for only 9 percent of the year's promised benefits.

Predictable proposals to raise the tax rate have come forth, but this course of action would have a brutal effect upon our economy. Taxing enployers more for Social Security (which, of course, comes out of the real income of each worker) means increasing the cost of doing business, which in turn is passed along in higher prices for all the goods and services we buy, and which also makes American manufacturers less competitive abroad. Moreover, in times of inflation higher Social Security taxes place a greater burden on every worker, particularly the poor and those who are trying to care for or assist their aged parents. Higher taxes also fall especially hard upon those with large families.

Still others suggest that the taxable Social Security wage base be raised to $24,000 to avoid higher taxes on lower-income groups, a proposal that would remove $2808 in pretax income from persons earning $24,000 or more—an imcome group already hard hit by higher income tax rates. Needless to say, the impact would be even worse for working couples in the middle-income ranges.

Today, slightly more than three workers are supporting every Social Security beneficiary. By the year 2025—based on current population trends—the ratio will shrink to only 2.2 workers per beneficiary.

Clearly, then, the Social Security system—in addition to all other federal social welfare programs—is in need of major structural and procedural change. Fundamental, drastic alterations are long overdue. To begin with, future increases in Social Security taxes and benefits must be substantially held down, with benefits only for certain needy income groups being raised substantially.

Many people who are receiving Social Security, shouldn't. Today, a married retired federal civil servant with an annual pension of $8000 could receive a minimum monthly Social Security benefit of $140.70. If he lives, say, ten years and the benefit is raised annually by 5 percent a year in cost-of-living increases, he'll collect over $21,000. But this man could have contributed to the Social Security fund as little as $11.50 total (matched by his employer). Declared former Representative Martha W. Griffiths, "In this day and age, the minimum benefit for that couple is sheer waste."

People who are comfortably fixed and can provide for themselves and their families upon retirement, retired civil servants, military retirees, and other amply provided pensioners both inside and outside the government should be ineligible for such minimum benefits, or, for that matter, for regular benefits. Social Security should be tied to need wherever possible.

In a time when life expectancy has considerably lengthened, the arbitrary retirement age of sixty-five is totally unrealistic and a cruel punishment to millions of men and women who still have many productive years to offer. The retirement-eligibility age should be raised to sixty-eight or seventy, a move that would add billions of dollars to Social Security reserves by postponing the time when funds must be paid out in benefits.

I have no easy solutions to the welfare mess. But I have a few ideas that are worth considering and may point the way to some sensible alternatives to the course we are now on. Quite obviously, we cannot go on funneling money into open-ended programs with no maximum limits. We must place "caps" on all existing social welfare spending programs. President Ford proposed a 5 percent ceiling on future benefit hikes, but Congress rejected his proposal. Inevitably, we will find—as did New York City—that there is a limit to how much private income can be taxed away for transfer to others before the threads holding our economic system together begin to come apart. Specific ceilings have to be placed on what each and every social welfare program can commit itself to, with careful scrutiny by Congress each year to determine whether the figures need to be adjusted upward—or downward.

We've seen how the food stamp program has gotten completely out of hand. There are some steps that could bring it back within reasonable limits. Eligibility, for example, should be based on a person's gross income rather than net income, as is now the case. After subtracting questionable deductions, families with incomes of $14,000 or more can now receive food stamps. Strikers and students from well-to-do families have also been able to receive them. These groups should be eliminated from the rolls and strict limitations placed on allowable gross income and assets so that only the very needy are eligible. Such limitations would save billions of dollars and allow for an expanded food stamp supplement for the neediest Americans. The proposal that recipients be required to sign the coupons upon receipt and then countersign them when used, much like traveler's checks, would significantly reduce their abuse on the black market.

Finally, we've got to break out of the tax-and-spend syndrome into which we fall whenever confronted with a social ill. Most often, government cannot alleviate a given social problem by removing more money from the earnings of Americans and sending part of it back via a multitude of public assistance programs. The problem of the aged is a case in point.

America's aged now receive an estimated $76 billion from various federal programs and additional billions in state and local funds (Medicare, Medicaid, food stamps, Social Security, Supplemental Security Income, veterans' pensions, federal retirement benefits, "meals on wheels," public housing). But the growing problems of inadequate care for the elderly remain, and a growing body of evidence indicates they're worsening.

Meanwhile, a proposal of Senator James L. Buckley of New York rather refreshingly looks to another approach that does not include welfare. Senator Buckley suggests a $1000 tax deduction for any taxpayer who provides, free of charge, in his or her residence, housing for anyone sixty-five or older, whether related or not. His proposal—I would at least double the tax deduction—looks not to the state, nor to the institutionalized facilities that bureaucracies instinctively look to as the way out of almost any social dilemma. It would go a long way, I think, toward moving the problems of the aged away from public assistance "solutions" and back toward individual and family responsibility.

One cannot discuss America's burgeoning welfare state without laying to rest once and for all some insidious superstitions, one of which says that America is pouring the great bulk of its public resources into a gluttonous defense establishment. The fact is that "human resources" programs have exceeded defense spending since 1971 and now make up over 56 percent of the total federal budget.

And studies show that rather than the rich getting richer and the poor getting poorer, low income families aren't doing too badly. One HEW study showed, for example, that because of Medicare and Medicaid, low-income groups spent more per capita on health care than middle- and upper-income groups. Families earning under $6000 a year spent $360 for health care in 1970. Families with incomes between $6000 and $11,000 spent $247, while those with incomes over $11,000 spent $294.

Meanwhile, one cannot escape the conclusion that rising health care costs today are caused by expanding federal intervention into medical practices, which diminishes the incentives of health care providers to hold down costs as government over-inflates demands on health care resources. Former HEW Secretary Weinberger agrees that "the faulty design of Medicare and Medicaid is the principal culprit responsible for the super-inflation of health care costs."

And if anyone is in doubt as to the efficiency of government in the health care field, he would do well to remember a General Accounting Office study that found that it costs the federal bureaucracy almost twice as much as it costs private insurers to process each Medicare claim. The GAO found that this is because federal employees are paid more and do less work than employees of private insurance firms. The GAO also discovered that the government is also far slower in paying claims than the less-costly private insurers.

What we must begin to recognize is that continually raising taxes in order to transfer income and provide social services for needy and low-income individuals has not significantly raised the standard of living of the poor. Think of all the hundreds of billions we have spent in tax monies at the federal level alone to try to eradicate poverty, and then consider figures from the Bureau of Labor Statistics that show that those within the lowest 20 percent income range had an estimated 5.2 percent of the total money income in 1965 and that that percentage had crept up to only 5.5 percent by 1973. Something is wrong here, and Washington apparently doesn't want to recognize it. Income redistribution to aid the poor isn't working.

What we need is not income redistribution but job distribution that gives the poor enough earned income to provide for themselves. And jobs are provided, as we discussed in the previous chapter, when government controls the urge to take a larger share of the national income and instead leaves a greater share of that income in the economy to be cycled into capital investment, expansion, and ultimately jobs and higher salaries.

The tax resources of Americans are not unlimited. Americans want to help, but they want their money to help the really unfortunate, not those who can and should shift for themselves. And one can understand the enormous resentment many welfare programs engender among a large segment of Americans when they see that little has changed for the better despite all the hard-earned billions they have relinquished to the tax collector.

We've tried declaring a war on poverty and have unleashed an army of social workers on the deprived and underprivileged. But the slums remain, the poor are poor, and the bureaucracy, programs, laws, and supporting taxation all continue to grow and proliferate. At some point we have to try another approach. The question is, when?

V

Crime

Lock Them Up!

Americans by the millions are being terrorized, looted, maimed, mugged, murdered, raped, and vandalized. Like inflation, the crime rate rises every year. Yet it is only in recent years that crime has been virtually going through the roof. Our country can truly be described as under seige and, tragically, little is being done to effectively reduce crime and to keep criminals off the streets.

According to statistics compiled by the Federal Bureau of Investigation, serious crimes rose more in 1974 than in any previous year on record. More than 10.1 million serious crimes occurred in 1974, about 1.5 million more than in 1973, an increase of 18 percent. "Serious crimes" include murder, robbery, rape, assault, burglary, theft, and auto theft.

The FBI's compilations for 1974 showed that criminals—striking nineteen times every minute—took over 20,000 lives and stole property worth some $2.6 billion. The 1974 increase in crime was the biggest in the fourteen years records have been kept, and it was probably the biggest increase in history. There were 4821 crimes committed per 100,000 persons, nearly one crime for every twenty persons in America. The crime rate was far higher in the major cities, 5621 crimes for every 100,000 inhabitants.

Alarming increases were found in juvenile crimes, too. Juveniles under eighteen accounted for 27 percent of all arrests in 1974. Over the past five years, arrests of young girls under the age of eighteen went up 21 percent. Arrests of juvenile boys under eighteen increased 15 percent. Ten percent of the 16,000 persons charged with killings in 1974 were under eighteen. About half of those arrested for burglaries, larcenies, and car thefts were teenagers. Seventeen percent of those charged with assault, nearly 20 percent of those charged with rape, and almost one-third of those arrested for robbery were under eighteen. An astounding 31 percent of the offenses in the seven serious crime categories were charged to teenagers. Police arrested 1.6 million teenagers in 1974.

Enough people were killed in 1974 to populate a good-sized town, while thieves stole enough loot to pay the Justice Department's budget, more than twice what it would cost to run the city of Chicago for a full year. Nearly ten out of every 100,000 Americans were murdered in 1974, up 4 percent from 1973.

The cost of all this to the citizenry is now some $20 billion a year, according to a report by the Advisory Commission on Intergovernmental Relations. And there are other less tangible costs. For as the commission pointed out, "Fear of crime is destroying some of the basic human freedoms which any society is supposed to safeguard—freedom of movement, freedom from harm, freedom from fear itself." Thus, we are witnessing a country in which citizens possess almost 100 million firearms and people fear to walk the streets or use public recreational facilities.

The figures are menacing enough, but the statistics we have show only part of the problem. It is estimated that something on the order of only one-half to one-third of all crimes are reported to the police. And then there's the further factor that it takes on the average a year or more between indictment and trial for most criminal cases in most major urban areas. The crime problem is further compounded by a 40 to 60 percent recidivism —repeat offenders—rate. Attorney General Edward Levi succinctly boiled down this dismal evidence with the blunt observation that the figures "represent a tragic failure on the part of our present system of criminal justice."

America is in the undertow of an enormous crime wave. That much is clear. But why isn't something being done about it?

Something is being done about it, to the tune of over $4.2 billion since 1968. It is the Law Enforcement Assistance Administration, a classic example of government trying to throw billions of dollars at a problem in the hope it can be bought away. Perhaps not since the antipoverty program of the mid-1960s has any other government program been as wasteful and ineffective as LEAA. For all its billions and for all its programs, crime continues to soar.

An internal Office of Management and Budget memorandum complained that LEAA's billions have frequently been spread too thinly to be effective, all too often have gone for the purchase of "unnecessary [police] equipment," and in many cases have financed irrelevant projects at the state and local level. The memorandum, a preliminary study on LEAA's effectiveness, said the agency's "funds have been used for projects which have little or no relationship to improving criminal justice programming, funds are so widely dispersed that their potential impact is reduced, the absence of program evaluation severely limits the agency's ability to identify useful projects and provide for their transfer, and too frequently LEAA funds have been used to subsidize the procurement of interesting but unnecessary equipment."

How is LEAA fighting crime? Millions of dollars have been spent for consultants to write fat reports and studies few people will ever read or see but which somehow convey the belief that government is doing something about crime. Loyola University in Los Angeles, for example, was given a $293,700 grant to study the need for a looseleaf encyclopedia on law enforcement, an undertaking which produced a two-volume report that by any stretch of the imagination could not be construed to have contributed anything to the fight against crime. LEAA has funded research by a University of Toronto (Canada) teacher about crime problems in the United States to the tune of $67,822. Former District of Columbia Police Chief

Jerry Wilson received $48,465 to help him write a book about crime in the District as part of a two-year $163,828 research project intended to survey ten years of crime fighting in the nation's capital. The agency threw away $17,481 to have Press Intelligence Services, Inc., a Washington news clipping service, clip and send it stories about LEAA. Another $32,477 went to an Arlington, Virginia, visual arts firm to do the art work for a six-volume report of the National Advisory Commission on Criminal Justice Standards. LEAA even paid others to write its own annual reports. One Washington writer received $99,330 to prepare four of the agency's seven annual reports. And, hard as it may be to believe, LEAA spent $650,000 on a study to find out why people move from neighborhoods where the crime rate is high.

The incredible waste in this program is stunningly illustrated by one $541,623 grant "to promote physical fitness in police officers." LEAA planned to spend an estimated $200,000 of it for a vast array of exercise equipment and other medical devices. LEAA Administrator Richard W. Velde—who has publicly acknowledged that "there has been waste in our program"—wanted to develop a Dick Tracy–type wristwatch that would have allowed police officers to obtain a quick reading of their blood pressure, temperature, and pulse rate (in addition to telling time) while on the go. The $200,000 pipedream project was quickly abandoned after it was exposed by columnist Jack Anderson.

America's premier program to combat crime has become a shockingly wasteful, bureaucratically inept fiasco. Despite the expenditure of billions of dollars, LEAA has been run with few restrictions and little guidance or control by top Justice Department officials. Its block-grant program for state and local crime efforts, according to one Senate study, has been characterized by "inefficiency, waste, maladministration, and in some cases corruption." Since its creation under the Johnson Administration in 1968, LEAA has spent tens of millions of dollars, perhaps hundreds of millions, on dubious research and study projects that have had no tangible effect on crime fighting, but have fattened the income of a number of consulting firms.

Others, too, have benefited under this costly program, as Sen. William

Proxmire has pointed out: "The police hardware industry has been booming. Sales of radios, helicopters and riot gear have never been better. The consulting business particularly has done exceedingly well. The sad fact about LEAA is that it has encouraged states and local units to be more creative about winning federal grants than about combatting crime."

After three separate studies to attempt to determine what effect if any LEAA has had on crime, the General Accounting Office came up empty-handed. One of these studies found that "LEAA and the states have established no standards or criteria by which some indication of results or failure can be determined." In another report, the GAO said that despite LEAA's creation to develop "innovative new programs to combat crime, the agency was merely a source of federal funds for ongoing efforts."

The dismal failures of LEAA are at once tragic and ironic. The agency was created on the misplaced notion that if the police were given enough arms and enough sophisticated equipment, they could overwhelm criminals with superior force. But as LEAA's budget rose each year, so, too, did crime—in every major category. The figures were up another 18 percent in the early months of 1975. An estimated 37 million Americans each year are the victims of crime. Clearly, LEAA has been an abject and total failure.

What, then, can be done? Much has been said about the need for change in our criminal justice system. Certainly change is urgently needed. But I find that the so-called reformers, as with most reformers, want to change everything at once. They want a speedier criminal justice system as well as a reformed correctional system. They want higher paid police, judges, and prosecutors. They want the most elaborate police communications devices and law enforcement equipment that money can buy. In other words, they want whatever resources society can muster, and a good deal more, to be applied—however thinly—across the length and breadth of the criminal justice problem. It won't work. We've got to take our most immediate and critical problems first, deal with them effectively, and then move on deliberately and systematically to each new task on a priority basis.

And the first task to be tackled in the war against crime is curbing the spiraling crime rate. Considering that since 1968 violent crimes in the United States have lunged upward by 57 percent, it is becoming painfully apparent that, despite the old FBI slogan, crime does pay. The terrible truth is that our softly applied criminal justice system is allowing ninety-five out of every 100 crimes to go virtually unpunished. For every 100 crimes committed, only twenty are known to result in an arrest, while only seventeen of those will result in any charges being brought against the accused. Moreover, of the seventeen charged, seven will be referred to juvenile court, two will be acquitted, one will be fined, one will be convicted of a lesser offense, three will be placed on probation, and three will end up in prison. And of the three imprisoned, only one will serve more than half of his original sentence.

"No wonder criminals are running wild," declared Arizona's Rep. John B. Conlan. "There is almost no chance, under current odds, that a guilty criminal will get caught or go to jail." In one eight-month period in 1974 a special Boston police crime-fighting unit arrested 636 persons for violent crimes. Yet, amazingly, only 7 percent of them were given jail sentences of any substantive duration. Even more frustrating is the crushing statistic that 97 percent of all adults arrested in New York City for felonies are processed through the criminal system without a prison term. A mere 6 percent of persons with a serious prior record charged with burglary in Los Angeles in 1972 ended up in jail.

Clearly, our criminal laws must be reformed so that anyone committing a serious crime faces the absolute certainty that he or she will go to prison. We must enact mandatory minimum sentences. One way we can immediately make an enormous dent in the crime rate is to come down particularly hard on those criminals responsible for most of the crime in America: the repeat offenders. They are identifiable; they pass repeatedly through our beleagured criminal justice system, only to return again and again to the streets to commit still more crimes.

The rising crime rate could be substantially and permanently reduced if repeat offenders were virtually guaranteed under the law to be given heavy and progressively stiffer prison terms based upon the seriousness of the offense and the number of their previous offenses. Punishment for violent crimes of murder, rape, aggravated assault, robbery that results in serious bodily injury, burglary, heroin trafficking, and any crime committed with a firearm or other dangerous weapon, must be meted out uniformly and severely—without probation or parole. And we can no longer afford to allow prosecutors to permit criminals to "cop a plea" in an effort to ease court caseloads, returning hardened criminals again and again to the streets. The odds must be materially shifted against the wrongdoer. Strict, mandatory sentences for violent and other serious crimes, in addition to harsh and substantially lengthier sentences for repeat offenders, would virtually reverse America's ascending crime rate.

Such an idea is not a particularly new one. It has been treated at length by such august and unlikely periodicals as the *New York Times* and endorsed by various Justice Department officials, including Assistant Attorney General Richard L. Thornburgh of the Criminal Division. In an address to the Wisconsin Chiefs of Police Association, Thornburgh observed that part of the problem with our correctional system has been "the impulse in some quarters to try to 'correct' all offenders. Much time and effort can be wasted in efforts to rehabilitate repeat violent offenders, major racketeers and the like. These offenders should be subject to predictable and certain terms of incarceration—if for no other reason than to protect the community from their depredations during their time in jail."

Liberals, too, are slowly coming around to the realization that something drastic must be done and that the old slogans about first curing the root social causes of crime are not enough. Even Senator Edward M. Kennedy concedes now that liberals can no longer "counter law-and-order slogans with arguments that crime can only be controlled by demolishing city slums, ending poverty and discrimination . . . let us not confuse social progress with progress in the war on crime."

Kennedy, in fact, is urging that "we start making punishment and imprisonment for violent offenders a certainty," which he says is "the most effective way to deter potential offenders from criminal conduct. At the same time, mandatory sentencing keeps the violent offender in jail and off the street."

I think the crime rate could be slashed if we instituted mandatory minimum sentences under which criminals committing felonies would get at least a year in jail, crimes of violence would merit a minimum of four

71

years imprisonment, repeat offenders would receive double that sentence, and crimes committed with a firearm or other dangerous weapon would automatically be punished by a minimum five years in prison. And no probation or parole.

Beyond this giant step to combat crime, there can be no doubt that our antiquated and creaking judicial system is in need of major overhaul and that its procedures and judicial machinery must be brought into the twentieth century. We will not win the war on crime as long as our courts continue to process criminals the way they did 100 years ago. Modern management innovations and computerized data processing methods must be rapidly introduced into our courts if they are to deal effectively and efficiently with the crushing backlog of cases that is engulfing them. Congress has moved on a program of speedier justice at the federal level, but the program is sorely underfunded and without adequate direction.

Can there by any doubt what would be the state of our prosecution and conviction rate if a major share of the $4 billion we have wasted on LEAA had been poured into improving our judicial and prosecutorial machinery? The emphasis in federal support must be shifted from police helicopters and walkie talkies and other flashy machinery to the nuts and bolts procedures through which criminals are put behind bars. The problem is not catching criminals, but convicting and imprisoning them.

Additionally, we should begin redirecting both our laws and our law enforcers away from what can only be considered marginal crimes that serve to overburden our police, crowd our courts, and add enormously to the cost of our prison facilities. Pot smokers, vagrants, drunks, and drug addicts should not be clogging our criminal justice system. Rather, they should be handed over to some lower-level noncriminal court established solely to find help for such individuals through the appropriate government and voluntary social service agencies. Our courts and police would thus be freed to deal swiftly and surely with what they should be concentrating on—the rapists, murderers, muggers, and thieves.

Finally, there can be no doubt that our prison facilities must be upgraded, expanded, and improved so that criminals—particularly young first offenders—who can be reformed are segregated from hardened and irredeemable criminals. The enormous cost of maintaining the kind of enlarged prison population I'm suggesting—whatever its magnitude —would be worth it to a society substantially free from the fear of crime.

Nonetheless, taxpayers cannot be asked to carry the entire burden in order that criminals may pay their debt to society. The cost of paying the debt is becoming astronomical. It now costs somewhere between $10,000 and $20,000 a year to maintain each prison inmate in America. Perhaps we should begin thinking in terms of requiring convicts to shoulder some of the cost of keeping themselves behind bars.

What I have in mind is combining the largely unresolved problems of criminal rehabilitation with the growing problem of allocating sufficient public funds to adequately staff and maintain effective prison systems. In other words, why not put America's criminals to work in productive, profit-making enterprises run totally within prison confines. The earnings of such enterprises would accrue to each state treasury to help pay for the cost of maintaining our prisons (with perhaps a certain percentage going either to the inmate upon release or for the living expenses of his family, who in most cases must turn to welfare).

There are a number of light industries that could be profitably run within expanded prison facilities, perhaps by the state itself or under contract with the private sector. The electronics, garment, furniture, and ceramic industries come most notably to mind as excellent possibilities. Private companies engaged by the state to establish and run the businesses would teach their trades to prison inmates cleared to participate in the program. The company would probably get a superior product at a relatively low cost. The state would share in the profits a number of ways, not only in the additional revenue to maintain each state's prison population but in the virtually free vocational training and rehabilitation the program would provide to largely unskilled, untrained, and unmotivated individuals. Upon leaving prison, ex-convicts would have a trade and a work record plus some accumulated earnings. Certainly that is better than the traditional new suit and some pocket cash. Perhaps the very firms that employed them on the inside would be eager to employ them on the outside at a considerably higher salary. The chances of ex-convicts returning to crime and to prison would surely be considerably lessened, perhaps eventually reducing our large prison populations.

While much remains to be worked out under such a program, certainly it is preferable to put our imprisoned criminals to work rather than having them—as is now largely the case—vegetating in their cells, dwelling on their incarceration, bitter, hateful, lonely, bored. At any rate, it is worth a try.

There are no quick solutions to the crime epidemic that is sweeping America. But there are some bold steps we can take to dramatically halt the spread of crime. The federal government is presently spending something on the order of a billion dollars each year in "revenue-sharing" funds to help states and localities improve their criminal justice systems. Tragically, the billions of dollars Washington has thrown into the bureaucratic and wasteful excesses of the Law Enforcement Assistance Administration have failed to alleviate the crime rate. We do not need to spend hundreds of millions of dollars to study the causes of crime. We do not need to spend millions on surveys and reports that only gather dust on some bureaucrat's shelf. We know what causes crime. We need to spend that money and more to deal with it. That means a speedier criminal justice system that can efficiently try and convict the guilty.

LEAA's inability to bring about even a modest downward movement in the crime spiral—even a fraction of a degree would be welcome—should have been recognized by Congress long ago. LEAA could produce the most modern police force in the world, but unless we provide our courts with the resources to do their job efficiently and fairly, crime will continue to be on the ascendency. Former District of Columbia Police Chief Jerry Wilson has perhaps best expressed the need for different priorities:

> As police officials, we know that unless the man on the beat is backed up by a system of vigorous prosecution, prompt trials, and rehabilitation programs that produce results, then the criminal will sooner or later be back on the street to cause more problems for society and for us.
>
> The fact is that making police more effective is wasteful—if society continues to permit the overburdening of judges and the clogging of courts.
>
> And increasing the number of judges is futile—if courtroom administra-

tion is not modernized and the number of prosecutors and defense attorneys remains inadequate.

And an expanded judiciary cannot take advantage of realistic sentencing alternatives if new correctional facilities and programs are not provided.

With one American household out of every four being hit by crime, the time has come for the implementation of fair but severe justice. Yet, despite the critical need for changes in our system of criminal justice, they will not come unless the people themselves begin far more vigorously to demand them.

VI

Education

Back to Basics

Despite the expenditure of nearly $100 billion a year at all levels, there has been an alarming and rapid decline in the quality of education in America. By every measurable test, our schools are turning out students who cannot adequately read, write, or compute basic mathematical problems.

Perhaps in no other area of government activity can one find more disturbing examples of bureaucratic mismanagement, misdirected policies, wasteful and ineffective spending, and a seeming obsession for experimentation solely for experimentation's sake. The evidence is everywhere for all to see, yet year after year Congress mechanically approves multi-billion-dollar aid-to-education bills without seriously questioning whether or not many of the programs being funded are necessary, effective, or proper.

Consider the evidence. The scores of high school seniors on College Board Scholastic Aptitude Tests have been plunging to new lows in a steady twelve-year decline. In 1975, SAT scores dropped ten points on the verbal test and eight points on the math test, the sharpest drops since the decline began in 1963. The year's average scores were also the lowest since computing of SAT averages began in the middle 1950s, with a forty-four point drop on the verbal tests since 1963 and a thirty point drop on the math tests.

The decline in SAT scores is highly significant because it reflects what is happening to the high achievers in our education system. There has been a consistent drop in scholastic achievement over the past dozen years—with the most dramatic drop occurring among our brightest children.

Some educators argue the decline is due to the increasing number of students taking the college boards. But their case has been convincingly disputed by analyst Frank E. Armbruster in a 300-page government-financed study published in August, 1975, by the Hudson Institute. According to Armbruster, if one accepts the educators' theory, the absolute number of top-scoring students should stay about the same or even go up somewhat. In fact, what has happened, he says, is

> that the absolute number of students scoring between 750 and 800 (the highest possible score) also seems to have decreased. In the year between 1972 and 1973, the number of male high school grads scoring between 750 and 800 on the verbal portion of the test declined from 1,573 to 987.
>
> Second, while it is true that the number of test-takers increased in the 1960s, from 933,000 candidates in the 1962-63 school year to 1,606,000 in 1969-70, the number of candidates declined to 1,354,000 in 1973-74. Yet the scores continued to drop. During this period, the verbal aptitude scores dropped at about twice the rate of the mathematical scores, but both plummeted at a faster rate than they had during the prior five years, when the number of students taking the test was increasing.

What makes this downward trend in scholastic achievement all the more alarming is that it is occurring while astronomical sums of money are being poured into education. Expenditures at the local, state, and federal levels on both public and private primary and secondary education rose from $6.7 billion in 1950 to about $61.6 billion in 1974. Yet despite this almost tenfold increase, student enrollment didn't even double, rising from 28.6 million to 49.7 million. Incredibly, while elementary and secondary student enrollment rose from 42 million to 49.7 million between 1960 and

1974—a rise of only 18.3 percent—education expenditures went up from $18 billion to $61.6 billion, a gain of 245 percent! Public schools account for the largest portion of this expenditure: $56 billion in 1974 to educate some 45 million school children.

The plunging SAT scores are not the only evidence of the decline of American education. A number of studies show that the writing skills of teenagers have declined over the years. For example, in 1974 the National Assessment of Educational Progress surveyed the writing skills of 80,000 students aged thirteen and seventeen, comparing them with samples taken in 1970. The results showed that over a four-year period writing skills had significantly deteriorated, trending toward shorter "primer-like" sentences, simpler vocabularies, and awkward and incoherent sentences and paragraphs. While the study found spelling and punctuation about adequate, there was a "drastic drop" in coherence and a trend toward fragmented sentences.

A recent U.S. Office of Education study revealed that more than 23 million adults do not possess the basic know-how to function effectively in our society. The study confirmed a survey by the National Assessment of Educational Progress, which found that many young people lack the basic mathematical skills needed to function as consumers. The U.S. Office of Education found that 29.4 percent of American adults were incompetent, while 33 percent were found to be barely competent to answer basic consumer economics questions. U.S. Education Commissioner Terrel H. Bell called the study's findings "rather startling" and said they "call for some major rethinking of education on several levels."

For years the decline in basic educational skills has been most evident at the college level, where teachers have consistently complained about the poor reading and writing abilities of incoming freshmen classes. But their complaints went seemingly unnoticed at secondary education levels, and the scores on college boards and other exams continued to drop to their presently pathetic levels. "The verbal skills of students have gone down incredibly in the last 10 years," declared Dr. Shirley Kenny, head of the University of Maryland's English Department, where the basic freshman English composition program was changed in an effort to teach students verbal skills they should have mastered in high school.

79

The disastrous failure of today's educational policies was amply illustrated at the University of Wisconsin, where 125 out of 200 students who took an English usage exam in 1975 in order to qualify as majors in journalism failed. According to Wisconsin English Professor William Lenehan, "students are not convinced they need to know how to write. But they really do need to know how." While the failure rate on the exam in 1975 was 60 percent, it was only 30 percent the previous year and only 25 percent in 1971.

Dr. James Kinneavy, director of freshman English at the University of Texas, blamed the plunge in test scores in part to a "dialectical tolerance" among high school English teachers trained in the "new linguistics." According to this theory of teaching, any ethnic dialect of English is considered just as good as standard English, and thus, the prevailing rules of punctuation and grammar are treated as unimportant. "There are enough teachers in high school who believe in this and are practicing it so that I think it's a factor," Professor Kinneavy suggested.

How is it possible that America could rise from a total national education expenditure of only $3.2 billion in 1940 to more than $96 billion today, and yet find its educational achievement going steadily down hill? What is going wrong here? Much of the problem, I believe, is that we have careened wildly away from some basic and proven educational concepts and blithely sailed off into the hazardous field of experimental education seeking new ways to educate our youth. We have subjected our youth to everything from new math to "dialectical tolerance" to open classrooms. The tragic result can be seen in the latest SATs.

Who fostered all this experimentalization? Much of it was born in Washington. As Congress poured more and more money into aid-to-education programs of all shapes and sizes, the U.S. Office of Education and other agencies frantically financed a vast maze of experimental teaching and curriculum programs. Many of the old tried and true educational methods were discarded—simply because they were old. So-called forward-looking educators insisted on "new approaches," "new concepts," "new attitudes" in education—in keeping with our "new" oriented society. Thus, broadly written education bills mandated the Office of Education, the National Science Foundation, and other agencies to "reform" American education.

Billions of dollars are poured into special studies and surveys on American education, which do little to improve the education of our children but a great deal to benefit lucrative consulting firms and research organizations that have become a major industry unto themselves, getting rich off annual education appropriations bills. An examination of the fiscal 1975 $25 billion authorization bill provides some choice examples of where our aid-to-education dollar is going. Conceding that reading achievment has sunk to new lows, the bill included a whopping $413.5 million National Reading Improvement Program under which the commissioner of education contracted with professional educators to evaluate the effectiveness of special experimental reading programs. How these tests of "special emphasis" reading programs were to improve the reading capabilities of our children is difficult to grasp. But the operative word here is "experimental" —as long as that is its thrust, Congress seems eager to embrace it. The reading funds included a total of $293 million for fiscal 1975, 1976, and 1977, the expenditure of which was mandated in some rather loose language. To wit: "participation of the school faculty, school board members, administration, parents, and students in reading-related activities"; "planning for and establishing comprehensive reading programs"; "preservice training programs for teaching personnel"; and "appropriate involvement of leaders of the cultural and educational resources of the area to be served." Predictably, as in almost all bureaucratically conceived innovations, the law requires each state educational agency to create an "advisory council on reading." The program authorized $3 million annually for reading programs on public television and $32.5 million over four years to fund special "reading academies" to be operated in part by government-selected community organizations and "nonprofit" groups.

Will all this improve the reading abilities of our children? I doubt it. Previous generations somehow learned to read quite well without such "innovations." We can, however, be confident of one thing: no one will try to evaluate whether or not such programs have effectively raised the nation's reading achievement level. The program—unexamined by Con-

81

gress—will just go on and on. And reading achievement will go down and down.

Another section of the fiscal 1975 authorization measure picked our pockets in behalf of women's liberation. That section authorized the commissioner of education to issue grants and sign contracts with public agencies and private organizations to develop and distribute profemminist "curricula, textbooks, and other educational materials," "pre-service and inservice training," "guidance and counseling," and other research and development programs including ones for "underemployed women." It included the establishment of a seventeen-member Advisory Council on Women's Educational Programs, which would play a significant role in the funding of these programs, including "a national, comprehensive review of sex discrimination in education." A victory for women's lib. But is it better educating our children? The inescapable conclusion is no.

Where else is our aid-to-education money going?

—A "Special Projects Act" under which the commissioner will issue lucrative contracts for "(1) new educational and administrative methods, techniques and practices; (2) to meet special or unique education needs and problems; and (3) to place special emphasis on national education priorities." The law promised $200 million a year to this vaguely drawn program, $10 million just to push the metric system.

—Fifteen million dollars a year in special projects for "consumer's education," again causing another expensive federal agency to be created, this time an Office of Consumers' Education within the U.S. Office of Education.

—Seven hundred and fifty thousand dollars a year for grants and contracts "to encourage and assist state and local educational agencies to establish and conduct programs . . . in the arts."

—Another $15 million "to demonstrate the most effective methods and techniques in career education," creating the new Office of Career Education, which is supposed to "foster flexibility in attitudes . . . in order to enable persons to cope with accelerating change and obsolescence." This tidbit created the National Advisory Council for Career Education, charged with conducting a nationwide survey of "career education programs, projects, curricula and materials."

82

—Seventeen million dollars annually to "provide educational, recreational, cultural and other related community services" and a "community education program," and creating still another advisory council to advise the commissioner of education in developing policy guidelines and regulations involving community education.

—One hundred and four million dollars over a three-year period to finance the new National Center for Education Statistics, including a seven-member Advisory Council on Educational Statistics.

It took forty pages of the *Congressional Record* to lay out this vast $25 billion aid bill, which President Ford signed into law.

What is clear from reading all the complexities in this program is that federal aid to education has gone far beyond its original intent. It is no longer a simple and direct program to aid the states and localities in pursuit of their own diverse educational needs. Years of congressional amendments and the broad program changes they brought about have fundamentally redirected federal educational aid. Our aid program has become a vehicle for social change, not for educational advancement and excellence.

In far too many ways, our public school system has become a vast experiment for federal programs, testing everything from psychotherapy to "environmental modification" (the Orwellian tag for placing children in foster homes).

A reading of HEW's *Pacesetters in Innovation,* which outlines federal elementary and secondary education aid programs, reveals the experimental depths to which the educationist bureaucrats plunged in order to find new ways to educationally mold and motivate our children. Described as a program "to support supplementary education centers and services, guidance, counseling and testing" at the state and local levels, the PACE (Projects to Advance Creativity in Education) projects run the gamut from "Behavior Modification" to "Psychoeducation Clinics" to "Changed Parent-Student Relationships" to "Total Environmental Control" to "Humanistic Curriculum" to "Sensitivity Training." So help me, one program described "experimental busses featuring multichannel programming, individual receivers and active response opportunities (allowing audio presentations of cognitive and/or affective [emotional] instructional materials)."

83

The program's scope is disturbing, not only in its intent to bring about deep changes in the very fabric of our society, but also in the way it seeks to force "behavior modification" upon our schools through thousands of on-going behavioral research projects financed by the federal government.

Far more comprehensive in scope and to a large degree more dangerous, is the growing role of the National Science Foundation in developing, marketing, and promoting controversial school curriculum materials that have had an unhealthy influence on our school children. NSF has funneled more than $160 million to a relatively small group of "career curriculum innovators" who have had a devastating effect on American education, fostering the disastrous new-math concept and filling our public schools with a repertoire of new teaching materials, many of which harbor strong political biases.

For example, since 1958 NSF has spent some $17 million on the new-math concept to teach our youngsters abstract theories in mathematics instead of the essentials of how to add, subtract, divide, and multiply. The result, as surveys indicate, has been an entire class of young people who are incapable of performing such basic mathematical exercises as balancing a checkbook and computing a weekly salary.

Dreamed up at a small NSF-sponsored conference of educators, the new math was pushed into the schools despite the fact that it had not been adequately tested to measure its ultimate effect on students. Numerous educators have pronounced it a total failure. For example, Morris Kline, a New York University mathematician, believes the new math should have been thoroughly tested in pilot programs before NSF glutted the curriculum marketplace with teaching materials and promoted the approach's use among state and local education officials. "Instead, they just rushed the stuff into the schools," Kline said. "It was irresponsible educational innovation."

An equally tragic example of NSF's follies in the school curriculum field is its MACOS (Man: A Course Of Study) program for ten-year-olds. Developed, marketed, and promoted by NSF at a cost of over $7.4 million, this course deals in part with the Netsilik Eskimo culture. This part of the course depicts killing female babies and the elderly, wife-swapping, and incredible visual and written scenes of violence, such as this one from a story about an Eskimo woman who murders her daughter out of incestuous desires: "As time went on, the old woman grew angry, for she too wanted a husband. She envied her daughter more and more, until one day when Kiviok was out hunting caribou, she killed her. She pulled the young smooth skin from her daughter's face and hands, and with it she covered her wrinkled, old face and bony hands."

The MACOS films and reading materials, which have beem used in 1700 fifth-grade classrooms, are unnecessarily graphic in depicting gory scenes of animal killing, the eating of raw flesh and organs, and sexual activities. Educators have testified that the materials have had harmful behavioral effects on highly impressionable ten-year-olds. Dr. Rhoda Lorand, a highly respected New York City clinical psychologist, had this to say:

> The program not only forces the children to be preoccupied with infanticide and senilicide, as well as the gory details of animal slaughter. It also aims at making the children accepting of these practices. Further, the children are forced to identify with the customs, through role-playing, even of Eskimo myths. In the enactment of one myth, a child about whom I was told was required to play the role of the elderly grandmother who clings to a boat which is about to leave her behind to die. Another child was assigned the role of her offspring who chops off the grandmother's fingers so that she cannot delay their departure. . . .
>
> It is incredible that this exercise in sadism should be foisted upon a captive audience of children who are undergoing the crucial process of adaptation to our culture and civilization. Equally incredible is the fact that a program so lacking in awareness of children's emotional development and needs, as well as in the purposes of education and the processes of character development, should ever have been given government support.

The so-called Individualized Science Instructional System (ISIS) is getting started in some 110 schools around the country. Designed to replace basic science courses for students who don't want to take them, the courses offer brief two-to-three-week "mini-courses" on sex education and socioeconomic subjects, with a decidedly pro–big government philosophy.

As an example of the kind of indoctrination such nationwide curriculum materials can perpetrate, here's a typical multiple-choice question from one of the ISIS exams:

> Besides providing love, food, and comfort, what other responsibilities do parents have for raising their children?
> a) Providing safety, religion, and prejudice.
> b) Providing religion, safety, and schooling.
> c) Providing safety, financial support, and mental stimulation.
> d) Teaching religion and providing a spouse.
> e) Providing safety, teaching religion, and providing a spouse.

The test guide gives as the only correct answer *c*, the only answer which rules out the teaching of religion as a responsibility of parents. Thus students are taught that parents either should not teach religion to their children or that it is not one of their important responsibilities.

It is frightening enough that the federal government is getting into school curriculum innovation in a big way. But it is even more disturbing to know that the government is subsidizing entire teaching programs without any determination as to whether they are needed in the first place and with little or no evaluation of their actual effectiveness. An investigation of MACOS by the General Accounting Office found NSF had "no guidelines for evaluating the effectiveness of educational products it supports or normal procedures for determining any adverse impact on human subjects using the materials."

The GAO also found that NSF went to extraordinary lengths to make their MACOS materials more marketable than those being produced in the private sector. For example, it lowered its normal royalty rate by 80 percent after fifty-eight regular textbook publishers rejected it. The GAO probe further revealed that student scores on MACOS tests were falsely represented in NSF promotional literature to make them look good, that the agency made no attempt to determine whether educational programs proposed by grant applicants were needed, and that NSF conducted no independent evaluation of its courses to gauge their merit before shelling out millions of dollars to promote them.

What all this means is that the federal government is moving increasingly toward more experimentalization in teaching methods and courses and playing a larger role in the development and application of school curriculums by innovators far removed from local school districts. Too often, Congress has tried to tinker and meddle with American education, mandating aid programs that require local education officials to depart fundamentally from basic educational practices and procedures. We are witnessing the sad result. Scholastic achievement is plummeting across the country.

Rather than trying to impose uniform educational policies, nationally mandated from Washington, we should instead be seeking and implementing a national educational policy that serves to maximize diversity in education through a multiplicity of approaches tailored to fit local needs and local resources. For starters, we should get out of educational experimentalization and school curriculum innovation lock, stock, and barrel and totally redirect our aid programs back to basic educational goals and practices.

We should gradually pare down and restructure the total aid program so that the bulk of the federal aid to education dollar goes not to America's wealthiest and most comfortable suburbs (as is now the case), but to the poorest and neediest school districts, particularly in our inner cities and rural areas.

We should institute a generous tax deduction for those Americans who choose to send their children to private elementary, secondary, or post-secondary schools.

And, finally, Congress should resist the temptation to undertake major educational "reforms" through vague and ill-defined programs that do nothing to fundamentally educate our children, yet unnecessarily swell the bureaucracy and waste billions of dollars. In short, our basic educational goal should not be to remold students or restructure our society, but—quite simply—to teach.

VII

Freedom and Privacy

What Have We Lost?

Freedom is not lost all at once, except, perhaps, through violent revolution. Liberties are lost bit by bit through a process of attrition often imperceptible to the general population—until it is too late.

Little by little, we are forced by the state to give up this freedom or that bit of privacy, all in the name of the public good. Americans are by and large obedient to the law, except when it tries to impose some moral imperative such as Prohibition. So we shruggingly, uncomplainingly accept each loss of freedom and invasion of privacy. We answer the prying questions of the Census Bureau. We fill out forms to comply with new regulatory requirements and procedures. We do not do business or engage in interstate commerce where the government says we cannot. We accept cars with maddening federally imposed buzzers that stop buzzing only when seatbelts are connected. We open our financial records at the whim of IRS agents. We comply with unnecessary federal safety-inspection demands. We cannot contribute more than $1000 to each political candidate we wish to support. We cannot raise air fares or freight rates without prior government approval. We cannot enter into voluntary agreements to privately deliver mail, even though this might be cheaper and more efficient than the Postal Service. The list of "don'ts" is excessively long, and it is growing. And we obediently go along, without question, without complaint, without challenge.

Meanwhile, our freedoms are being infringed upon in other, less obvious ways. The revelations of the last few years indicate that we may be the most spied-upon people outside the Soviet Union. Government has followed us, bugged our phones, intercepted our messages abroad, opened our mail, kept files on us, intimidated us, conducted counter-intelligence operations against us, and inflicted an array of other investigative-surveillance activities upon us through numerous agencies.

Many of these activities, conducted by several administrations over many decades, were legitimate national security and law enforcement tools. Some, however, went beyond proper limits. Parts of the FBI's now discontinued COINTEL program, for example, under which phony letters were sent to discredit Ku Klux Klan members and left-wing political activists, were not only ineffective but improper. On the other hand, we know that much of the government's infiltration of violent racist and political groups was proper and, at the time it occurred, necessary. And in some instances, the FBI's network of informants very often prevented violence and provided information that frequently led to the quick arrest and conviction of persons responsible for shootings and bombings in the South and elsewhere. Other programs also went too far, including indiscriminate letter openings and electronically scanned telephone interceptions that violated the freedom and privacy of honest citizens.

The inescapable conclusion from all the horror stories of the last several years is that government became as bureaucratically duplicitous and extravagant in the investigative-surveillance and intelligence fields as it had in so many other areas. After surveying the many activities of the Central Intelligence Agency, the National Security Agency, the Defense Intelligence Agency, the intelligence agencies of the armed forces, and other federal intelligence and investigative arms, it is quite evident that too damn much has been going on, much of it barely understood or monitored by Congress.

The righteous hue and cry by some members of Congress over America's intelligence activities proved nothing more than that Congress had suddenly awakened to the fact it had failed to keep an eye on all these programs, had neglected its responsibility to maintain proper oversight, and for years had approved money bills without questioning where all the money was going. If there were excesses, Congress has to bear the major share of the blame.

Further, Congress has not served this nation well by investigating our intelligence activities in the way it has, unnecessarily revealing the names of secret agents and exposing specific acts and programs, which has only served to weaken the credibility and intelligence capacity of America. We may never know the full damage done to our intelligence efforts abroad by the disclosures of the House and Senate probes. It remains to be seen whether Congress will reform the way our intelligence activities are conducted *and* monitored without sacrificing our ability to conduct covert operations necessary to the protection of our national security and the advancement of freedom around the world.

But beyond whatever blatant intelligence excesses that may have occurred, there exists a larger and more dangerous threat to our liberties. It's growth in recent years has gone largely unnoticed, yet its ultimate effect on the freedoms and privacy of all Americans could be crushing.

I refer to the rapid advances being made in computer and electronic technology and the giant strides undertaken by government to install the very latest systems for more effective and efficient control over its programs and, eventually, you and me. The increasing use by our national government of highly sophisticated electronic surveillance and information retrieval and storage systems poses enormous dangers to our most fundamental liberties. Without fanfare, Washington's growing bureaucracy has been systematically developing a vast computer network that is capable of coding and cross-coding the names and numbers of almost every man and woman in America. A portent of things to come may be found in a survey that discovered that fifty-two out of sixty major federal agencies had conducted some form of electronic monitoring of their employees.

Electronic communication systems can now scan thousands of telephone calls indiscriminately and, triggered by a precise programmed code, pick out and record specific calls. The Vietnam War brought us the first operational use of the "electronic battlefield," by means of which the movements of people were monitored. Related advances have been made in the field of medical science in the development of devices to monitor patients constantly wherever they may be. Law enforcement agencies, seeking broader control over entire populations to more effectively combat crime and terrorism, are integrating computer networks on a national scale to enable the instantaneous transmission of information.

We may not have reached the "plague of surveillance" decried by California's Sen. John V. Tunney during a hearing on the subject, but we are certainly approaching a situation in which a network of sophisticated space-age surveillance and data maintenance technologies is engulfing traditional concepts of freedom and privacy. It no longer shocks us, for example, to learn that our highest officials, including presidential candidates, have been bugged. We are not surprised to hear a Supreme Court justice say that the nation's highest court, and even the president of the United States, have been kept under electronic surveillance. No wonder a national poll found that more than half of the American people believe "things have become more repressive in this country in the past few years."

Dr. Jerome B. Wiesner, president of the Massachusetts Institute of Technology, is among those who believe the situation has reached "crisis" proportions because a growing "information technology puts vastly more power into the hands of government and private interests that have the resources to use it" and that "to the degree that the Constitution meant for power to be in the hands of the 'governed,' widespread collection of personal information poses a threat to the Constitution itself."

Forseeing even more "significant changes" in the development of computer and communications technology—both in equipment and in highly sophisticated programming to perform complex information processing tasks—Wiesner is understandably alarmed. "These trends," he says, "if not counteracted, mean that it will become increasingly attractive to use computers and communications networks in complex surveillance systems and to program the networks to carry out sophisticated sorting correlation, and other search procedures to identify and keep track of subgroups of the population with special characteristics."

Warning of an approaching "information tyranny," in "the innocent pursuit of a more efficient society," Wiesner told a joint hearing of two Senate subcommittees:

Many practices that pose long-term threats to democratic government and personal freedom are being, and will continue to be inaugurated because they provide a means of making the society function more effectively. The exchange of computerized credit information and the exchange of criminal data are examples of this. The ever-increasing scale of industry and matching growth in the size of government are also examples. Many serious students of the social scene question whether it will be possible to preserve our democratic institutions in the difficult time ahead.

Some sociologists, Wiesner continued, believe that this

overriding commitment to efficiency implicit in technological society has meant from the start that the "needs" of the system, the society, would inevitably be given priority over the rights of the individual, and that it was only a matter of time before the democratic processes could not handle the evolving situation. This is the central question of our times.

And what happens when government places the efficient management of society above all else? Based on the experiences of other countries that have chosen that path, Wiesner says he can reach no other conclusion but that

overmanagement of a society actually reduces its effectiveness, that centralized control works considerably less effectively than our form of industrial democracy for managing a technological society. One can see the effects of over-control in our own country. Regulations, needed or desirable for one purpose or another, have almost always restricted the ability of the regulated industries to innovate and respond to changing conditions, and thus in many cases have made further controls necessary that in turn introduce further inhibition on adaptation and so on.

A central problem in all of this, and one which Weisner only touches upon, is the fact that a huge, all-consuming government will by its very nature seek to maximize and make more efficient the control and power over those it governs. The growth of government in itself spawns the Big

93

Brother syndrome that is at the very heart of an advancing Brave New World technology.

Bear in mind that for government to implement and execute universal programs, several factors must be present, not the least of which are various degrees of compulsion and the application of massive amounts of control data. As government equips itself to become technically more efficient through advanced technology, its authority and power must similarly grow. And that is what those of us who prize individual freedom and privacy should fear most.

Eventually, we must decide just how big and how powerful and how efficient we want our government to become. We have to decide just how far we want to go to compel people to achieve certain social goals, no matter how desirable they might be.

Not too long ago, the Senate voted on a bill that would have dealt with the shortage of doctors in our more rural areas by compelling medical school students upon graduation to practice at least two years in a rural area. The measure was overwhelmingly defeated, but the philosophy behind that bill—compulsion by government—remained behind to rear its head another day. For it is in Congress, where our laws are fashioned, that our precious liberties can be taken from us, bill by bill.

That is why John F. Kennedy once warned that "the scarlet thread running through the thoughts and actions of people all over the world is the delegation of great problems to the all-absorbing Leviathan—the state. . . . Every time that we try to lift a problem to the government we are sacrificing the liberties of the people."

More recently, former HEW Secretary Caspar W. Weinberger observed that "apart from its sheer magnitude, federal spending has shifted toward programs that reduce the remaining freedom of individuals. We are creating an edifice of law and regulation that has intruded into the lives of all of us—both those it seeks to help and those who do the helping. The entire human-resources field is under the lash of federal law—doctor, hospital, teacher, college president, student, voluntary agency, city hall and state capital."

Government can perform great works for its people. It is also capable of great tyranny. An industrial democracy such as ours cannot long endure

94

under the crushing weight of government controls, surveillance, and regulations. Our system can continue to work and to function only when the people have the maximum degree of freedom possible. Through legislation, government regulations, and other encroachments our freedoms and privacy are slowly being diminished by the state. We will not sacrifice an orderly and lawful society by discarding those restrictions upon individual freedom that are unnecessary and improper, or by requiring that future laws or programs or regulations meet the strict test of need *and* be consonant with a free society.

We need to have a great debate in this country about what we want in our government, how much of it is needed, and how much control we are willing to relinquish over our daily lives. The pendulum in our society is swinging toward heavier and more elaborate government controls and less and less individual decision-making. More and more, government is deciding how we should live our lives and how our money should be spent. Sadly, it is no exaggeration to say that we are today faced with hard choices not very different from those that confronted our revolutionary forefathers 200 years ago. As the tentacles of government compulsion and invasion of privacy grow stronger and tighten their grip on all of us, we must eventually answer the question too many want to ignore: how much freedom are we willing to give up, and for what purposes?

VIII

Defense

Will We Be Ready?

Liberals like to place all government spending into two distinct categories—defense and "social welfare"—as if maintaining America's defenses had nothing whatsoever to do with people's welfare.

But nothing is more relevant to America's welfare than military spending, for it protects the United States, its people, and its democratic form of government from foreign domination. Our military defenses allow us the luxury of living free from the fear that our country can be taken over by an outside enemy. For 200 years America's military establishment has delivered the most effective welfare program in recorded history. We remain a free nation, our shores untouched by foreign invaders.

Lest we forget, America's defense is the primary responsibility of its government. This above all else must be borne in mind as we engage in a Great Debate over just how much military preparedness is enough. The point is easily overlooked as military critics argue that America can lay aside much of its conventional weaponry and stop developing more effective strategic weapons without endangering its security and the security of

97

the free world; that world conditions are such that America can afford to substantially reduce its defense budget; that defense spending has grown too large and that wasteful and extravagant spending exists only in the Pentagon and nowhere else in government; and that we can maintain an effective and efficient military posture with outmoded aircraft, missiles, and naval vessels.

Federal defense spending is admittedly high—$90 billion for fiscal year 1976 alone. But America's military spending is proportionately nowhere near what it has been in the past. Between 1952 and 1972 Defense Department spending increased from $46 billion to $77 billion, 66 percent over twenty years. Meanwhile, spending on health, education, and welfare rose from $5 billion to $85 billion, an increase of 1346 percent! Put another way, total federal spending increased over those twenty years by $158 billion, but of that sum 51 percent went to Health, Education and Welfare, and 19 percent went to Defense.

The Great Lie, repeated over and over again by critics of military spending, is that defense spending has been growing by leaps and bounds, out of all proportion to the federal budget. Just the opposite is the case. Year after year, we have been reducing the Defense Department's share of the over-all budget, while social welfare spending has been going through the roof.

President Ford's 1976 budget request for the Defense Department was $94 billion (Congress approved $90 billion), a figure that captured the big, black headlines of the nation's press. Compare that sum with the $118.4 billion that Ford requested for HEW, the new Goliath of the federal government.

In 1952 military spending represented 49 percent of all federal outlays, some $46.6 billion. It rose to $80.5 billion by 1968, consuming 45 percent of the budget. But for fiscal 1976, Ford's $94 billion request represented only 26.9 percent of the total budget. This was in sharp contrast to the roughly $150 billion spent in the same year on a variety of social welfare programs, including social security, health care, unemployment compensation, welfare assistance, and food stamps, which consumed 42 percent of the total budget.

Now, $90 billion is a tremendous sum of money. Yet the fact remains

98

that defense spending has fallen considerably below Cold War levels. Defense budgets have increased, yes, but the increases have in no way kept pace with inflation. We have had to cut military forces in order to pay our military men more. We have had to buy fewer weapons in order to obtain costlier and more sophisticated arms.

A burgeoning, uncontrolled military? Hardly. We now have 585,000 fewer persons under arms than we did in the pre- Vietnam year 1964. Each Army division has been reduced from 59,600 men to 48,700. Navy ships have been cut from 917 to 490—the lowest level since 1950. Overseas forces have similarly been declining, from 719,000 in 1964 to 480,000 today.

A skyrocketing defense establishment that has run amok? Far from it. Ford's budget request for fiscal 1976 included 271 fighter attack planes, compared to 583 ten years ago, a reduction of 59 percent. It also recommended two new attack submarines, compared with six in 1965, a 66 percent cutback; it asked for 138 new helicopters, compared with 1226 in fiscal 1965, a 90 percent drop; and it included no new transport aircraft, compared with 84 in 1965, a 100 percent reduction.

And what have the Soviets been doing during all of this, pray tell? They have been steadfastly increasing military spending and enlarging their military forces and arsenals.

Since 1964, Soviet military manpower has risen by one million men, to double the strength of U.S. military forces. Between 1972 and 1974 the Russians have produced on the average of 3000 tanks a year, while the United States produced an annual average of 462. They have manufactured 1200 artillery pieces a year, in sharp comparison to 170 a year for the United States. They produced 930 tactical aircraft a year; we turned out 540. They built thirty-nine surface ships per year, while we built only eleven.

In the category of strategic aircraft, the United States has 450 B-52 bombers, of which 241 are G and H models, modern low-altitude penetration bombers, plus 76 of the newer FB-111s. The Soviets possess 140 heavy bombers and 1200 refuelable medium-range aircraft.

The growing gap in strategic missiles is, however, far more ominous. The United States possesses a total of 1054 intercontinental ballistic missiles (ICBMs)—450 Minuteman IIs, 54 Titan IIs, 550 Minuteman IIIs —and forty-one missile-firing submarines, of which thirty-one are equipped with a total of 496 Poseidon MIRV (multiple independently targeted reentry vehicles) submarine-launched ballistic missiles (SLBMs) and ten with a total of 160 Polaris single-warhead SLBMs.

The Soviet Union has 1518 ICBMs, of which 313 are in the heavy-missile class, with the remainder in the "lighter" classes. The Soviets have a total of fifty-five nuclear powered, missile-carrying submarines, all built after 1964, with an additional twenty-two older diesel-powered submarines capable of launching nuclear-tipped missiles. All together, the Soviets have 750 sub-launched missiles of both the MIRVed and single-warhead types.

Comparison between the missile capacities of both superpowers is complex and difficult. But the key to measuring American versus Soviet strategic strength is each side's "throw weight" capacity, the amount of explosive tonnage—or payload—each missile force can deliver on enemy targets. For some time the Soviets have possessed a throw weight advantage of approximately four to one. By 1975 that advantage had grown to six to one. By the time the Soviets have completed replacing their current ICBM force with the new, more powerful SS-17 and SS-19 ICBMs —which they are permitted to do under the SALT I agreement—they will have installed a land-based missile payload capacity of 11.7 million pounds, while we may have a capacity of only 1.1 million pounds, if we phase out our Titan IIs and single-warhead Minuteman IIs in the mid-1980s. In other words, the Russians will be able to deploy about ten times as much firepower on their ICBM's as we have presently.

As this is written, our negotiators have made no attempt to obtain a reduction in the number of the larger Russian missiles being deployed under the SALT I accord.

Beyond the Soviets' rapid strategic build-up, there is the equally disturbing question of Russian violations and exploitation of the SALT I disarmament agreement. The evidence is everywhere. Former Defense Secretary James R. Schlesinger has stated repeatedly that the Soviets have violated the terms of the agreement. In a *Reader's Digest* article, former Defense

Secretary Melvin R. Laird wrote flatly, "The USSR has violated agreements to limit strategic weapons." A top Pentagon official privately informed a reporter that "we have been unable to detect any indications of Soviet restraint" in the development of heavy payload missiles that "have the potential for becoming first-strike weapons because they endanger the survivability of deterrent forces." The respected American Security Council recently published a declassified Defense Intelligence Agency report (written in August 1975) that observed, "Whereas in the U.S. detente tends to be seen as an end in itself, in the USSR it is seen as a strategy for achieving broader Soviet strategic objectives as well as tactical aims." Other specific, unattributed evidence of violations has appeared in the usually reliable *Aviation Week and Space Technology* and even the liberal *New Republic*. Senator Henry M. Jackson of Washington, highly respected in the Senate for his penetrating knowledge of defense questions, says bluntly that SALT I is "full of loopholes which the Soviets are actively exploiting in a massive build-up of their nuclear arsenal."

Senator James L. Buckley of New York, who has devoted a good deal of his time and energy in the Senate to Soviet–United States defense questions, stated in 1975 that "the Soviets have violated major portions of the first round accords to the point where it is clear that any future agreement must be fully verifiable. No reliance whatever can be placed on Soviet good faith." Among the violations, Buckley lists these as among the most serious:

> They have attempted to prevent verification of their compliance with the terms of the SALT I accords through concealment, camouflage, clandestine experimentations, and other techniques, all in violation of Article XII of the ABM treaty.
>
> They have deployed a new generation of ICBMs which are approximately 50 percent larger than permitted under the definition of 'light' missiles provided the Senate during hearings on the SALT I accords.
>
> They have conducted a clandestine program to upgrade their air defense system to an ABM system. They now have in place the SA-5 system consisting of high-powered transportable radars and 1100 launchers, each with six reloads, which has benefited from more than 60 illegal ABM experiments.

Important details about the Soviet submarine construction program [are] now being concealed so that we may not be able to reliably determine, among other things, whether or not . . . Soviet submarine[s] [are] being equipped with multiple warhead missiles.

Under the 1974 Vladivostok agreement the Soviet Union and the United States were each allowed no more than 2400 nuclear missiles and strategic bombers. Of that total, only 1320 missiles were allowed to have MIRV warheads. But, instead of adhering to these limitations, the Soviets have been enlarging their strategic power. And there is little doubt that they are going for a nuclear first-strike capability.

The payload advantage aggressively being pursued by the Russians is not what Congress had in mind when it approved the Jackson amendment to the ratification of the 1972 SALT accords, which calls for nuclear parity between the two powers under any future agreement. Yet what has been happening is that the United States has been slipping into a position of nuclear inferiority, a position from which we can only bargain from weakness.

This weakness in our bargaining position became quite evident when our negotiators at SALT II did a complete turnabout and accepted the indefensible Soviet position that their supersonic Backfire bomber was designed solely for use over the Eurasian land-mass and not for intercontinental attack. Instead of counting the Backfire among the Soviets' strategic nuclear delivery systems, we weakly agreed that the aircraft—which carry the new AS-6 air-to-surface missile—would not be counted for offensive strategic purposes, unless they are based at Arctic airfields on the USSR's northern rim closest to the North American continent. The speciousness of that deal is obvious. The Backfire can on very short notice be deployed at these northern bases, and the AS-6 can reach every important target within the United States at up to 2.5 times the speed of sound.

In light of the fact that the Soviets are upholding neither the spirit nor the letter of the SALT I agreements and are instead expanding both their conventional and strategic forces, what should be our defense policy as we enter America's third century? To begin with, we can no longer afford to

102

engage in a debate over America's future military security by mouthing outdated criticisms and posturing long dismissed arguments.

For instance, it cannot be denied: there is enormous waste in the Defense Department. From a bloated civilian bureaucracy of one million (to support 2 million uniformed personnel) to an extravagant pension system to ineffective and costly reserve programs to an endless chain of fringe benefits, the degree of waste in the military is sizable and totally unnecessary. Like every other department in government, the Defense Department is a victim of bureaucratization. An incredible 53 percent of our defense budget went for personnel costs in fiscal 1976, not for weapons development or procurement.

The existing system of compensation for our military forces provides a cornucopia of benefits from cosmetic plastic surgery for women to free warehouse storage for retirees. Our military, depending upon rank, can receive free or subsidized housing, free legal services, free travel on military aircraft, reduced interest rates on home mortgages, and a pension equal to 50–75 percent of base pay upon retirement (which, luxury of luxuries, can arrive as early as age thirty-seven). There once may have been legitimate reasons for many of these benefits, to compensate our military men in time of war, or when salaries were low, or when they were forced to move frequently from one base to another. Martin Binkin, a senior fellow in the Brookings Institution's Foreign Policy Studies program, concludes that "the system used today to compensate armed forces personnel, a system geared to meet the needs of the military establishment of an earlier era, is a costly anachronism."

The burgeoning costs of health and pension benefits are cutting more and more deeply into the defense budget each year. "And if the present course is continued," Binkin says, "these two programs, which in themselves accounted for over $9 billion, or about 10 percent of total defense spending for fiscal 1975, will probably consume a growing proportion of the total budget for military manpower." In sharp contrast to the government's civilian employees, the military contribute absolutely nothing to their pensions. Requiring that they do could cut defense costs by up to $2 billion annually.

103

With the steady and successful implementation of the all-volunteer military force and significantly improved salaries and training programs to lure young men and women into the service, there is no longer any justification for military commissaries that sell tax-free, cut-rate (20 percent off) groceries with the help of a $440 million-a-year federal subsidy. Senator William Proxmire has been raging against this one for years: Uncle Sam employs more than 8400 servants to serve at the beck and call of our highest military brass as well as junior Navy and Marine Corps officers—at a cost of over $90 million a year.

In addition to eliminating the foregoing wasteful activities, here are some other cost-cutting proposals that make eminently good sense:

—Reducing Army troop levels by 200,000 men at a savings of almost $2.5 billion a year, which would still provide the United States with twelve active duty Army divisions.

—Thinning out a top-heavy bureaucracy of officers brought about by the military "grade creep" that promoted lower grade officers simply to raise their salaries. The Pentagon says the 1972 combined total of 18,138 colonels, Navy captains, generals, and admirals, was 1000 more than the number of high-ranking officers serving America in 1945 when we had 14.7 million men and women under arms.

—Prudently reducing nonessential Defense Department civilian personnel. Defense now has as many civilian employees as the departments of Health, Education and Welfare, Treasury, Agriculture, and the Postal Service combined.

—Extending the average military tour of duty (for every month the average tour of duty is extended we could save $200 million annually) for a possible savings of up to $2 billion a year (this would require the adoption of standard three-year enlistments.

—Our active Army, Army National Guard, and Navy reserves could be cut by up to 25 percent without substantially diminishing the military preparedness of our armed forces by placing those discharged in a nonpaid, standby reserve pool to be called in the event of a national mobilization. Reservists with whom I have talked privately confess that weekend training drills have become lax and wasteful exercises that do not substantially contribute to America's defense.

—A stringent review of unneeded military bases and facilities both abroad and around the United States, leading to a gradual closing down of those found to be unnecessary to our defense or the defense of our allies. There is a potential savings here of over $1 billion.

These are some areas where defense spending could be significantly reallocated and reduced without compromising or weakening our overall strategic and conventional strength. The proposals could be lengthened with a laundry list of smaller expenditures that pad the Pentagon's budget and consume tens of millions of dollars annually. Why, for example, should our top military brass be provided special dining rooms where they may dine on steak dinners at cafeteria prices, with the taxpayer picking up the difference between the real cost and the menu's cut-rate prices. Why should wives of military personnel be provided with free face lifts, nose jobs, and breast enlargements by military plastic surgeons at the taxpayers' expense? Why, indeed, should taxpayers be asked to shell out $14 million a year to operate and maintain 300 military golf courses both here and abroad?

But having said all of this, we must again face the unimpeachable fact that America's defense must be the first priority of the federal government. The United States—if it is to remain a free country, unintimidated by any power, great or small—can never afford to be anything but number one militarily. This is not only important to our country but to all the other nations of the free world—and those who wish to someday be free—who see the United States as the last guardian of world freedom.

Thus, while I would substantially curb this nation's wasteful and unnecessary "defense" expenditures, I would continue—and even raise somewhat—whatever expenditures are necessary to keep the Soviet Union—and any other foreign enemy—at bay. This will not be an easy or inexpensive task as the Russians deploy heavier MIRV missile systems, develop a larger version of their nuclear missile submarine, harden their ICBM silos, and produce a new intercontinental bomber. In the face of all this, we can neither afford to retreat into a Fortress America nor to fall behind militarily. Continued development of the B-1 supersonic bomber, the Trident submarine, and other more sophisticated and efficient weaponry must receive top priority in our defense budget—even at the

105

expense of other less vital components of our defense structure—if we are to thwart the Russians from overtaking us militarily.

At the same time, there are portions of our defenses that are in need of serious review, with an eye toward substantially directing our military resources away from such largely outmoded and enormously costly systems as the Navy's nuclear-powered aircraft carriers. About 50 percent of the Navy's annual $26 billion budget is poured into these supercarriers, which are becoming increasingly vulnerable to the Soviet surface fleet's new antiship missiles. Each of these Navy dinosaurs costs $2 billion to build, consuming a total investment of $5 billion when outfitted with aircraft. There's something wrong with our ability to sensibly evaluate and invest our limited military resources when we see the Russians putting the bulk of their resources into nuclear-tipped "arrows" while we continue to drop $5 billion apiece into nuclear-powered "canoes."

One other major area of distorted spending that comes under the defense budget is military aid. It has grown large and wasteful and can no longer be ignored. We spent a total of $4.5 billion in fiscal 1976 on military aid and credits of all types, sprinkling arms around the globe to nations both large and small, friendly and unfriendly. I, for one, believe that much of our military aid program has gotten dangerously out of control. Much of it is totally unnecessary and in the long run can only heighten world tensions and fuel future conflicts. I would like to see our arms-aid program slashed to the bone, with the United States providing military assistance to only a select few countries that meet a severe test of need.

Americans want a national defense that is impregnable. This sentiment is clearly demonstrated in national polls, which have consistently evidenced a lopsided prodefense position among our people. But Americans also want to see their defense dollars spent wisely. They want an end to inter-service rivalries, which too often involve promotion of pet programs without any hard evaluation of their relative merits. Americans would like to see a day when the world can be more peaceful and when the major powers can negotiate an honest curtailment of the arms race. But they accept the world's realities and the nature of man for what they are. They are not deceived by Soviet rhetoric when matched against Soviet armaments. Asked in an Opinion Research survey, "Do you trust the Soviets to keep the Strategic Arms Limitation Treaty even though there is no provision for on-site inspection by either side?'' 74 percent of the respondents said no, while only 21 percent said yes.

Asked if the United States should maintain a military strength "greater than that of the Soviet Union," 76 percent answered yes and only 21 percent said no.

Americans are not fools. They do not trust the Soviets to keep their promises because they have seen them break so many previous agreements. They have always harbored a strong yet healthy distrust and suspicion of Russia's Communist leaders, and they have seen nothing in the USSR's latest policies and actions to make them change their mind, irrespective of what some American policymakers have done or said in the hot pursuit of détente.

I think it's possible—provided the Kremlin substantially changes its international policies—to someday seek a true reduction—not just ceilings—of arms. But the United States must provide the Soviets with the incentive to seek such a reduction. Cutting back our defense capabilities while the Russians continue to increase theirs is neither fiscal responsibility nor a sane "reordering of priorities." It is gambling of the most reckless sort. And this nation and the security of its people are the stakes. For myself, and I think for the vast majority of Americans, those stakes are too high.

IX

Foreign Policy

In the Real World

Within the past decade American policy toward the Soviet Union and her Communist allies has shifted from containment to détente. There are valid reasons to fear this change and the ultimate consequences it may have for the security of the United States and the remaining free nations of the world.

Genuine détente with the USSR is something every American would like to see achieved. However, there are important questions we must begin asking ourselves about détente: Does détente in fact exist today? Can détente ever exist so long as the Soviet Union pursues its expansionist policies?

We would all like to see Secretary of State Henry Kissinger's "stable international order" become a reality. In such a world, there would not only be a true balance of power between the Soviet Union and the United States but a common ground of mutual respect on which the two superpowers could achieve a gradual lessening of tensions through honest negotiations, eventually leading to a real arms reduction.

Secretary Kissinger's "grand design" for a "new structure of peace" is a noble and worthy—though highly idealistic—goal. Even so, we should ask ourselves whether the pursuit of this goal is based on the world as we know it is or as we wish it were. Are we seeking détente with the Soviet Union on the basis of our adversary's words, while ignoring our adversary's actions?

Surely no one would disagree that the pursuit of a stable world order is a highly desirable goal. What we must ask, however, is whether the goals and foreign policy of the Soviet Union have changed enough to make possible such stability.

Defenders of détente are extremely vague when responding to this pivotal question, for no rational observer of the world today can reach any other conclusion but that the Soviet Union's internal and external policies and goals have not in any fundamental sense changed for the better. Russia's police state has not softened; its declared "war" against the West still goes on. "Wars of national liberation" are pursued with continued aggressiveness. It is not the Communists who have changed, but, in many respects, our leaders' perceptions of them.

In his 1957 book, *Nuclear Weapons and Foreign Policy,* Kissinger bluntly branded the Soviet Union a revolutionary power and categorically dismissed the claim that the Russians were interested in "a basic and lasting accommodation" with the West. "That would be tatamount to asserting that the Soviet leaders have ceased being Bolsheviks," he wrote. "The only safe United States policy is one which is built on the assumption of a continual revolutionary struggle . . . our only possibility for affecting their actions resides in the possession of superior force."

The belief that the Soviets have since renounced their revolutionary struggle against the West and now seek a true accommodation with the United States would be tatamount to claiming that the Russian leaders have ceased being Communists. Kissinger, of course, no longer holds the realistic view he took in 1957, despite the fact that the Russians have by word and by deed never lessened their worldwide "revolutionary struggle," nor their moral and material support for wars of national liberation wherever they can be spawned and nurtured to fruition.

The record of the Soviet Union's escapades—and its successes—is both

110

impressive and disturbing. Heavy military aid to North Vietnam carried the Communists to victory after the fraudulent 1973 Paris peace agreement led America to its worst foreign policy debacle since 1812. Sustained financial and military aid to the Communist bloc in Angola has spun that country toward the Soviet orbit and could possibly provide the Russians with a naval base on one of the most strategic sea lanes in the West. Lavish aid to the pro-Communist military faction in Portugal has achieved a toehold on the European continent for the USSR. The Soviets also encouraged and prepared the Arabs for the war against Israel in 1973 and plotted with the oil-rich Arab states to cut off one of America's chief sources of oil and thus through blackmail force a Middle East settlement that would favor the Arabs. In addition, there is a sinister list of major and minor Soviet operations worldwide, including significant support for Communist parties and factions in France, Italy, Great Britain, and Third World and neutralist countries around the globe.

All of this and more has occurred since President Nixon carried the olive branch to the Moscow summit in 1972 and left hailing a new era in United States–USSR relations. It's a new era, all right. A new era for Soviet foreign intervention and military expansion. If this is the face of détente, then détente must mean something quite different to the Soviets than it does to us.

James Burnham recently wrote in *National Review,*

> For the Communist side, détente is not a "step toward peace," not a prelude to cooperation and friendship, but a mode of conducting the revolutionary struggle. It is not an effort to achieve an evenly balanced equation, but a maneuver to weight the equation more heavily against the West.
>
> Because of the strategic ascendency of Communism, it is "no accident" that in the successive détente episodes the Communist side invariably comes out ahead. SALT I turns out to be a green light for Soviet development of MIRV warheads and a stop sign for U.S. deployment of anti-missile defenses. The Vietnam peace accord turns out to be a program for completion of the Revolution along the Mekong; the big Soviet grain purchase, a ripoff of the U.S. farmers and consumers. The Helsinki accord becomes a guarantee against Western influence in Eastern Europe and a permit for Soviet-backed Communist operations in Western nations. Détente-blessed trade shapes up as the transfer of Western technology (and food) to make good the

failures of Communist technology in exchange for promissory notes and an occasional gold shipment.

For the Communists détente is a No Can Lose proposition. And détente has the special merit of providing an attractive packaging for Communist aggression. Who can be "against détente"?—against the lowering of tensions and the progress toward cooperation and friendship? Only obsolescent Cold Warriors or outright warmongers and fascists. Even if we did get a bit screwed at Geneva, Seoul, or Helsinki, all hearts are in the right place, and by nourishing the spirit of détente everything will turn out for the best in the long run.

The truth is that a considerable degree of delusion underlies our headlong pursuit of détente. Secretary Kissinger once wrote, "The West requires nothing so much as men able to create their own reality, for today we stand poised on a brink, tottering between unprecedented chaos and unparalled creativity." Our foreign policy seems based on the created illusion that if we make enough trade-offs with the Russians, allow them their victories in Indochina, Angola, Portugal, and elsewhere, formally recognize Russia's conquest of Eastern Europe in the 1975 Helsinki treaty, sign a so-called arms limitation treaty that virtually guarantees Soviet superiority in ICBMs and SLBMs, and then sweeten the deal with a batch of trade agreements and Export-Import Bank loans there will be peace.

The Soviets are now modernizing their strategic forces with several new more powerful, more accurate, longer range ICBM and SLBM systems. They are developing at least ten other strategic weapons systems. Can anyone watching this honestly say we are truly at peace?

Exactly what, after all our negotiations with the Soviets, have we come away with? What has our foreign policy provided the United States? When have we said that unless the Soviet Union and its satellites allow free emigration of their citizens, for example, we will refuse to sell them grain? When have we ever made further Export-Import Bank low-interest, subsidized loans a quid pro quo for getting out of Angola? Why were our trade negotiators unable as part of the 1975 grain purchase agreement to obtain a commensurate cut-rate deal on Soviet oil? Why is it that in every agreement with the Soviets we end up giving them more than they are willing to give in return?

112

Aleksandr Solzhenitsyn told a New York audience in 1975 that "the forces of the entire Soviet economy are concentrated on war, where you won't be helping them. But everything else which is lacking, everything which is needed to fill the gaps, everything which is needed to feed the people or keep industry going, they get from you. So indirectly you are helping them to rearm. You're helping the Soviet police state."

And we are. Can anyone deny it? From the first spare parts America supplied to Russia to rebuild its factories in the 1920s, to the automobile and tractor factories built during the first five-year plans, and into the postwar years to this very day—from fertilizer plants to textile factories—American aid continues. " . . . what they need from you is economically absolutely indispensable—not politically but economically indispensable to the Soviet Union," Solzhenitsyn informs us.

If Solzhenitsyn and other Soviet witnesses are correct, why are we economically fueling a country that is mounting the greatest military build-up in the history of the world? Why is it we are reluctant to say, "No, not another dollar of aid, or grain, or loans, or technical assistance unless we are provided with some concrete evidence that you have begun to curb your arms build-up and withdraw from foreign interventions"? Have we so lost our resolve that we are unable to hold to some basic human values and use whatever bargaining chips we may have to secure tangible gains in exchange for our largess?

It is on this very point that one discovers we have lost touch with some basic moral values in the foggy evolution of America's foreign policy over the last ten years. In our zeal for détente we seem to have neglectfully discarded our once proudly declared commitment to the principles upon which America was founded: human freedom, the dignity of the individual, and the inviolable sovereignty of the nations of the world.

The nations of the Communist world have existed in shackled silence for so long that we as a people have grown jaded and mute about their unending nightmare. Our capacity for anger and indignation about long-encrusted dictatorships seems to have softened and mellowed with the passage of time. The nation's store of outrage and despair and simple human sympathy for captive peoples everywhere appears to have been depleted. The days when we told those behind the Iron Curtain that they would not be

113

forgotten have become embarrassments in an era of dialogue over ways to improve and strengthen the very systems that keep the world's totalitarian chains locked in place. Thus, we signed the tragically deceptive Helsinki accords arising from the conference on European security and cooperation. What the Kremlin had been seeking since 1954—the "inviolability of national borders"—was achieved with the stroke of a pen; and the criminal Soviet enslavement of Latvia, Lithuania, Estonia, East Germany, Romania, Poland, Hungary, and Czechoslovakia had finally won the endorsement of the "land of the free."

In the bitterness and tragedy of the post-Vietnam era we are being consumed by an ostrich mentality, which variously lectures us to avoid the sweep of history and events, stay out of the internal affairs of other nations, stop trying to be policeman to the world, and say or do nothing in behalf of the repressed peoples of the world and those threatened with losing their freedom (lest we further inflame the passions of their oppressors). America does not have to be the world's policeman to fulfill her destiny to help preserve and extend freedom on this rapidly shrinking planet. We can no more ignore the onward rush of history and events in this nuclear age than we can fail to see the spreading blanket of repression and totalitarianism that is creeping over the continents of the world. According to the latest survey by Freedom House, a public-interest research group, as little as 19.8 percent of the world's population is truly free and 35.3 percent is only partially free.

But what to do about the 44.9 percent enslaved by totalitarian systems of one form or another? We can start with a foreign policy that declares that freedom is the paramount issue facing the world today; that totalitarian regimes—Communist or otherwise—will never receive the moral and material support of the United States unless meaningful steps are taken toward liberalization, e.g., freedom of emigration, freedom of religion, freedom of the press, freedom of speech; that America will never implement or pursue any foreign policy that may have the effect, economically or militarily, of strengthening any dictatorship's control over its people; and that this nation will not provide aid or loans or credit sales or assistance or cultural or technical exchanges to any country that materially supports military aggression against any other country. A clear and eloquent decla-

114

ration of such positions would again place America's foreign policy on the high moral plane on which it once stood.

There will be those who will call such a policy a return to cold war. But those making such a charge are likely to be the very people who have looked the other way for decades while millions behind the Iron Curtain and in Communist China have been executed or placed in concentration camps and psychiatric wards for daring to dissent. These are the very same people who have no trouble venting their rage on the Senate floor or at the United Nations against a country like Chile for its transgressions against individual freedom, waving a laundry list of sanctions that should be brought against the South American government. Yet these same easily outraged "humanitarians" fall strangely silent when, for example, India falls under the repressive heel of dictatorship. People who vociferously condemned corruption and persecution of political prisoners in South Vietnam are mute in the face of Indira Ghandi's corrupt regime and the mass jailings of all who oppose it. Senators like George McGovern can return wide-eyed from Havana calling for all sorts of concessions for the Cuban dictatorship, conveniently ignoring Castro's bulging prisons, the accounts of torture and beatings, and Cuba's involvement in another "war of liberation" in Angola. For the McGoverns of the world it is apparently easy to ignore the fact that almost half the world's population is not free. The double standards are endless, leading William F. Buckley, Jr., to ask, "What is it that accounts for the extraordinary success of the organized left in training the attention of the world on the Chiles of the world—while ignoring the Cubas."

Are we to continue to ignore these peoples—as our present foreign policy so cruelly does—even while we continue to do business with the very governments that subjugate them? Is that what America should stand for? Does simple morality and human decency have no place in American foreign policy?

Secretary Kissinger calls himself a "political realist," a man who believes he must act "on . . . intuition that is inherently unprovable" in order to reach decisions, not on the basis of facts, but through his own innate, mystical "vision of the future."

Political "realists" like Kissinger would prefer to continue America's

115

foreign policy as it is, dealing with a totalitarian world on its own terms and following history wherever it may lead us. But we can follow a more difficult policy, one that may be fraught with challenges and dangers, but one which sees the world for what it is—*and for what it can be*—and declares that the United States will use every legitimate economic, diplomatic, and military tool at its disposal to resist totalitarianism and to nurture and defend freedom.

When the Bolsheviks came to power they promised the Russian people bread and freedom. America is providing them with bread. There is still no freedom. In his 1975 New York address, Solzhenitsyn urged that the West allow the Soviet Union's socialist economy

to prove its superiority. Let's allow it to show that it is advanced, that it is omnipotent, that it has defeated you, that it has overtaken you. Let us not interfere with it. Let us stop selling to it and giving it loans. If it's all that powerful, then let it stand on its own feet for ten or 15 years. Then we will see what it looks like. I can tell you what it will look like . . . When the Soviet economy is no longer able to deal with everything, it will have to reduce its military preparations. It will have to abandon the useless space effort and it will have to feed and clothe its own people. And the system will be forced to relax.

America need not go to war to free the enslaved peoples of the world. Left to their own backward devices, their totalitarian masters will one day surely fall under the weight of their own unworkable, inefficient systems. In the meantime, we need not economically or otherwise give support to such governments. We need not sell or loan them the technical devices and know-how to make the machinery of repression more efficient and more powerful. We must allow them to fail.

One does not have to be a disciple of the domino theory to recognize the ominous trend of world events in the last few years. We have seen Laos, Cambodia, and South Vietnam fall into totalitarianism, the retreat of the West from Angola and Mozambique, the Marxification of Portugal, and the heightened Communist threat against South Korea, Thailand, the Philippines, and other nations.

There are those who counsel we should retreat from every corner of the globe and withdraw into a Fortress America. That would be alien to everything America stands for today. Too many nations still look to the United States as the last wall between themselves and foreign domination. If we falter, if we allow Soviet military strength to continue to rise far beyond that of the United States, then we shall surely see these nations fall one by one into the Communist orbit—either through internal seizure or through some form of self-preserving realignment under the prod of Communist threats and intimidation.

This kind of global domination by our adversaries can be prevented, but only by a United States willing to take the kind of diplomatic initiatives and build the kind of military muscle necessary to decisively swing the balance of power in a way that can maintain our freedom and the freedom of our friends and allies.

X

Some Final Thoughts

America is desperately in need of some fresh, new, unorthodox approaches to a lot of long-standing but not insoluable problems. But like bad habits, decades of inbred political prejudices are hard to break.

Year after year we have become locked into the same redundant public approaches to legitimate domestic concerns. Congress clings insecurely to inefficient, outmoded, and wasteful programs with an almost religious ferocity. Politicians, bureaucrats, journalists, businessmen, and educators alike are more often than not apologists for maintaining the status quo among federal regulatory and social welfare programs (with a few glaring exceptions that have more to do with political fashion than anything else).

Rarely does one find anyone in Congress—with power enough to do anything about it—asking if some of Washington's most entrenched public programs should not be scrapped or, at least, improved upon. Powerful interest groups fear trying new approaches or even going back to old proven concepts, lest they lose federal subsidies and other benefits in the process. Our lawmakers and bureaucratic managers have become addicted to the

119

public trough, believing that the answer to every problem is more federal spending—of our money. Every major organized sector of society either has or is seeking a pipeline to Washington—and into your pocketbook.

After over a decade of Washington watching, I am convinced that fundamental change is needed in our government—from the way it operates to the way it is structured. But I am equally convinced that the politicians and bureaucrats who now control the leadership positions in our government are virtually incapable of initiating and implementing such change. And the reason is that the sort of innovative approach to problems that is needed today is totally alien to their political-bureaucratic way of thinking. Politicians who have devoted their entire careers to applying the public sector approach to virtually every problem that comes down the pike, while bitterly criticizing the private sector for almost every national ill, are incapable of breaking out of their dim, narrow-minded ideological view of the world.

America needs visionary leaders and independent thinkers whose minds are not encrusted with conventional Big-Brotherish political prejudices. Government can play a valuable role in dealing with some of the nation's severest problems. But government is not the end-all for everything that troubles us. We have to begin looking elsewhere.

And one place we should begin looking is to private enterprise. The opportunities and challenges for the future are limitless if we can develop the kind of new ideas that will utilize business' unique incentives and modern management techniques to revitalize and, in many cases, replace failing government services and programs. Wherever possible we must use the energies and talents of the private sector, if only on a contractual service-for-hire basis, to operate public programs. Surely business can do no worse than government is now.

Consider two possibilities. With the Postal Service losing $1.4 billion a year and rapidly pricing itself out of the market, the private sector is still forbidden by law from competing for mail delivery business. Mail service is poorly run because there is no incentive to improve it. The bureaucrats who operate the mail service do so in the sublime knowledge that whatever debt they may incur, taxpayers will make good the difference through higher postage rates and increased subsidies from the Treasury. So the hard, competitive decisions that could offer lower costs, reduced rates, and better service will never be made. If IBM or Xerox were running the Postal Service, first-class postage would not be thirteen cents and climbing. And the mails would probably be delivered through the most technologically advanced electronic and computer systems available instead of the antiquated system we have now. If the Private Express Statutes—under which the Postal Service enjoys its monopoly—were abolished, businesses could enter the market and offer mail users—including the hard-pressed publishing industry—efficient alternative service at a far lower cost than today's Postal Service bureaucracy. Isn't the idea at least worth testing? Unfortunately, few in Congress are even thinking about—let alone proposing —this somewhat radical yet highly sensible alternative to a failure-ridden government operation.

Each year our Social Security system sinks more deeply into debt. Each year Americans are taxed more heavily to support it. And many are discovering that after all they and their employers contributed to the system—now up to a combined maximum of $1790.10 a year—they receive a mere pittance upon retirement.

Meanwhile, many economists and insurance-pension experts tell us that today's young workers could receive two to three times their predicted benefits under the present Social Security system if they were allowed to invest the same amount in a private pension plan. Despite all the deceptive rhetoric about it, Social Security is *not* an insurance system. The money taxed from your paycheck is immediately spent on payments to retirees and other benefits as soon as it comes in. There is no investment to allow individual tax contributions to grow with the economy.

Social Security has other drawbacks. For example, under its rigid rules the earnings of older workers between the ages of sixty-five and seventy-two are, in effect, taxed at a rate of 50 percent on income over $2760. Working wives receive less benefits than unmarried women workers. And the present payroll tax is so regressive that a majority of workers are now paying more into the Social Security system than they do in federal income taxes.

Several plans have been suggested by economists and others to provide Americans with a more lucrative alternative to the system we now have.

121

For example, under a proposed government-regulated plan, Americans would be provided with a choice of where their retirement "investment" would go. They could continue to place their payroll tax into a government-maintained fund, or they could opt to participate in a government-approved and monitored private insurance-retirement fund or a similarly approved bank-retirement program. If the charts and tables worked out by actuarial experts are correct, such alternatives can give the American worker an adequate retirement pension, ease his tax burden and that of his employer, raise his salary, and give the economy an enormous boost through the availability of billions of dollars in additional investment capital. At the very least, it is worth trying out, perhaps on a tightly controlled pilot basis.

But how many in Washington have dared to challenge this most sacred of sacred cows? The idea of providing safe, sane options to the government's compulsory system was once considered so radical that no politician would touch it with a ten-foot pole. Now, however, the concept is being seriously discussed outside of Washington by legal and financial experts of widely differing political outlooks. Eventually, Congress is going to have to give the idea serious consideration.

The Postal Service and Social Security are just two of the multitude of problems confronting government where the private sector can be used to provide Americans with essential services that heretofore have been considered the sole preserve of government. The business sector, through the incentives of the profit motive and the operation of market dynamics, can in numerous areas perform far more efficiently, equitably, and cheaply than can government. Perhaps the finest example of this was provided in a Columbia University School of Business study that found that because of "governmental inefficiency" it is cheaper to have your garbage taken away by a private firm than by a local government agency. In fact, the study found that the private sector could do the job 69 percent more cheaply than municipal collectors.

These and other free market approaches are not being widely discussed by Washington officials, who seem content with patchwork solutions and piecemeal reforms, allowing government to continue muddling along —growing bigger, costlier, less efficient, and more unresponsive.

Washington is growing ever more fat and lethargic, increasingly feeding off the earnings and energies of the private sector's—*your*—productivity. And those who dominate Washington's power centers find all of this exactly to their liking. For they are in the enviable position of deciding how all that delicious tax revenue—which is the stuff of power—is to be spent.

On the other hand, I'm beginning to sense that a more enlightened attitude is slowly beginning to coalesce outside of Washington—in what I like to think of as "the real world." Where once Americans eagerly looked to Washington for solutions to their problems, I find that more and more they are reaching the conclusion that *Washington is the problem*.

In a city that has been spinning furiously from scandal to scandal, it is easy to delude oneself into thinking that the nation is lurching along to the same savage drumbeat. One often finds, however, that it isn't. The blaze of CIA, FBI, IRS, and other headlines that have dominated the Washington scene throughout the middle 1970s really hasn't consumed anywhere near the same attention "out there" beyond the banks of the Potomac.

I particularly recall a trip to a small city on Maryland's Eastern Shore during the height of the CIA disclosures. This town is only two hours out of Washington. Upon arriving, I was surprised to find the city's daily newspaper had banner headlined across its front page a wire service story out of Washington which it, too, thought was a scandal. But the story was about a Government Accounting Office report that found four major regulatory agencies had spent lavish sums of money on overhead expenses such as furnishings, carpeting, and other office decorations, exceeding the overhead expenses of virtually every other agency of government. To this city's newspaper, this was the real scandal. In Washington or New York it barely was mentioned. Similarly, in city after city—far from Washington's noisy political posturing—I find that Americans are far more troubled and angry over what Washington *is* doing with their money than over what it is *not* doing.

We have just gone through one of the most turbulent chapters in American history. The news media have been fueled on high-octane events for several years, as we burned our way through Vietnam, riots, Watergate, impeachment, and assassination plots. Having been fed almost daily on the raw meat of scandal, it has been difficult for the media to settle down to the

123

somewhat more mundane matters of what our government should be doing and whether or not it is effectively performing in the public interest.

Wrongdoing in government must certainly be exposed. But I suggest that the media have by and large been ignoring what should be one of their primary tasks: monitoring what government is doing with our money. The federal government is gorging its way through a budget that is expected to reach $423 billion by the end of fiscal year 1977. Future spending projections place the next federal budget at upwards of $450 billion! Increasing deficits make future tax increases a virtual certainty. Yet, in light of all this, there has been little aggressive investigative reporting into where all this money is going and whether or not taxpayers are getting a dollar's worth of services for a dollar's worth of taxes.

There is incredible waste of taxpayer's money in Washington today, but there appears to be little news media interest in going after it. The subject isn't fashionable. "News," it would appear, shifts from issue to issue, like the seasons. And the media seems to follow it in packs. One day it is energy. The next, inflation. Then it is intelligence and spying.

But when will the media train its big guns on waste in government? What subject is more newsworthy and has more effect on the livelihood and welfare of all Americans than the enormous financial burden we must bear in the form of heavy federal spending and higher taxes? Think back over the last ten years and try to remember when any of the three major networks devoted a news special to the subject of rising government spending and its impact on taxpayers and the economy? You needn't try. There weren't any. Why is it that no one in the media has focused attention on the multitude of agencies and programs that proliferate in Washington and asked: Are they working? Are they needed? Are they affordable?

It is sad to report that Washington journalists—with rare exceptions—do very little in the way of questioning whether or not existing federal programs are operating to the public's benefit. Indeed, there is an innate tilt within the news media toward new government programs and an almost blind acceptance of ongoing programs and governmental institutions.

In brief, journalists in Washington are missing a story of major proportions: the waste of billions upon billions of tax dollars—*your* dollars—on

124

programs that are ineffective, inoperative, unneeded, or simply extravagant.

Washington contains a rich harvest of waste scandals, should any enterprising reporter or concerned group of citizens want to go investigating. And it is a story that is guaranteed to arouse the anger of our citizenry as even Watergate and the CIA exposes never really could. But it will take, I think, a far different approach to investigative reporting than we are seeing at the present time.

Reporters, in my opinion, must serve as the eyes and ears of the nation to draw its attention to wrongdoing and, through dissemination of the facts, to help correct abuses and spur necessary reforms. But in the search for public abuses and juicy scandals we may have lost sight of some equally important concepts and a few healthy suspicions. Governmental institutions and social programs are not untouchable. Government programs are enacted by men to spend the people's taxes for the country's defense and the general welfare. Somewhere among the scandals we have discarded one of the first responsibilities of Washington reporting: the ever-vigilant watch over and accounting of public funds for public purposes. It may not be as bloody or as filled with intrigue as Watergate or CIA activities, but uncontrolled, ineffective, and superfluous government spending is no less scandalous.

What Congress and the executive branch are doing with America's taxes—which now consume over 44 percent of all income—must become a higher priority in the print and broadcast media. It is a story that touches everyone's pocketbook and goes to the very heart of the economic health of our nation. Every now and then one hears proposals to create an all-powerful federal ombudsman who would oversee the government in behalf of the people and keep them informed of what's going on within the bureaucratic jungle. The American taxpayer already has a corps of ombudsmen in Washington. It is the press. But those who should be monitoring and exposing the wasteful expenditure of federal funds have been asleep on the job for too many years.